The

Young

Investors

Club

Table of Contents

Thank you to all my family and mentors.

This book is an appreciation for all the knowledge, wisdom, and guidance you have given me.

"Someone's sitting in the shade today because someone planted a tree a long time ago."

- Warren Buffet

Foreword

I met Suhas through an online networking event during the pandemic. We connected offline and I knew something was special about him.

No, it's not the fact he completed college-level finance coursework while in high school. And no, it's not that he was a DECA state champion.

I knew he was special because I could tell he genuinely cared about personal finance and that he cared about helping others, especially his teenage peers.

In this book, Suhas talks about many personal finance topics and places a large emphasis on investments. Investments are ultimately how one becomes wealthy, so it's important to learn these concepts if you want to become rich one day.

If you're a teenager who wants to achieve financial independence early in life, this is a must-read book! Suhas put together not only a book, but a guide on how to achieve financial independence.

If you're ready to learn and set yourself up for financial success, buckle in, and let's dive into the world of personal finance!

Vijay Kailash, CFA

-Derivatives Trader, and founder of OptionsSellingSecrets.com

Acknowledgement

In the process of crafting this book, it demanded over a year's worth of dedicated research and meticulous editing. The realization of this project would not have been possible without the invaluable assistance and guidance of numerous individuals.

First and foremost, I extend my heartfelt gratitude to my father, Badrinarayan Rajagopal Dhandapani, whose unwavering support and editorial expertise were instrumental in bringing this book to fruition.

I also want to express my sincere appreciation to Vijay Kailash, whose mentorship in investing, personal finance, and his gracious contribution of the foreword enriched this book immensely.

I am deeply indebted to my accounting teacher, Heather Baldwin, who introduced me to the intricate world of accounting and provided invaluable guidance throughout the writing process.

Furthermore, I extend my thanks to my economics teacher, Thomas Lefor, whose profound knowledge in economics greatly informed the content of this book.

Special acknowledgment goes to my marketing teacher, Jason Linnman, whose insights on writing style and content structure were indispensable in shaping the book's presentation.

I also want to express my gratitude to the members of the Oregon Young Investors Club, whose enthusiasm and inspiration were the driving forces behind the creation of this work.

This book stands as a testament to the collective effort and support of these remarkable individuals, and I am truly fortunate to have had their guidance on this journey.

Introduction: Why Should You Care About Investing and Finance?

When I talk to my friends about personal finance and investing, some of the responses are, "Nah, it's too early" or "I honestly don't care" or on the rare occasion, "My dad owns a business." It's responses like these that make me consider the importance of financial literacy. Just like math, it takes a lot of practice and knowledge to get good at something, even if it may be above us in years. Consider this: If you choose to start focusing on making money and saving after you finish college, you'll not only have student loans to worry about, but you'll also be dealing with living expenses and a lack of understanding about how to invest properly, perhaps putting your money in a safe and losing it to inflation. My friends' reactions to personal finance remind me of the importance of fiscal literacy. Don't wait until after college to begin learning about money management. Starting now will ensure a financially secure future.

If that doesn't pique your interest, learning how to save and invest money can help you afford things that may seem hard to get. For example, if you put $500 aside each month to buy a car, you will save about $30,000 over five years. However, in those five years, inflation will increase, as will the price of the car, meaning you will have to wait longer to afford a new car. The longer you wait, the more you will have to spend. A new BMW 3 Series costs about $45,000 before taxes with options today, but in 1990, the same car cost about $20,000 in today's money. So the longer you put money in a box under your bed, the more you will have to continue saving. But if you invest that $500 dollars in an exchange-traded fund (ETF), you can earn an average of 7% per year. With the magic of compound interest (which I will explain in a future chapter) at the end of the fifth year, you'll have $35,611 dollars compared to just $30,000. If you diversify your investments, you can make even more. This is just some of the magic I explain in the book.

Many people make money, but they have no idea how to use it. In elementary school, I had a friend whose parents worked very menial jobs, yet he would always come to school decked out in the latest fashions. I wondered why my parents shopped at Ross and always sought discounts. Curious, I asked them, and that's when they told me something I hold to this day: You should save and invest more than you spend. You see, if you make money, the government takes its share, and after that, you must pay expenses like rent, utilities, food, loan payments, etc. Not knowing what to do with what is left over is the cause of financial misery.

Did you know that money-related problems are the number one cause of divorce? It's one of the reasons why people sign prenuptial agreements and keep finances separate for a while. A person with poor financial skills can put a marriage in jeopardy and perhaps their family as well. If you want to have a family someday, then you will have to establish a budget and then live within it. Even if you don't want to get married or have a family, it is still going to be necessary to develop good financial skills. With no one around to correct you, it will become very easy to lose control of your finances and end up broke.

A little more than fifty years ago, the American dream was something very achievable—a blue-collar job, a nice house in the suburbs, a car, enough money to support a family, and enough to put your kids through college. In the United States, the average income is $56,000 before taxes (Semega, 2022). To give you perspective on how low that is, the average rent in the US is $1,794 dollars per month (Kodé, 2023)[1]. This means that having a place to live will cost you a fifth of your pre-tax income. The average price of college is now a little over $36,000 per year for a low-end state university (Hanson, 2023)[2]. Gone are the days of living on one salary while still having a house and comfortable amenity with a middle-class job. If you want that lifestyle, it will take at least $100,000 a year to sustain it. This is why having good personal finance skills is important—you can find ways to make do with what you have while also finding ways to make more.

[1] Kodé, Anna. "The Typical American Renter Is Now Rent-Burdened, a Report Says." *The New York Times*, 25 January 2023, https://www.nytimes.com/2023/01/25/realestate/rent-burdened-american-households.html.

[2] Hanson, Melanie. "Average Cost of College [2023]: Yearly Tuition + Expenses." *Education Data Initiative*, 6 September 2023, https://educationdata.org/average-cost-of-college.

Introduction: Why Should You Care About Investing and Finance?

You are considered very lucky if you leave college with a job paying $100,000 per year. If you're in a big company, it supposedly gets better because of benefits, retirement funds, stock options, etc. But they don't tell you how hard it is to progress from there. It usually takes a person fifteen years to go from an analyst (or equivalent entry-level position) to a vice president or managing director. This means that if you wait to get a raise, you will live the same lifestyle for fifteen years, unless you get massive raises. Combined with inflation, you will be saving to just maintain your lifestyle. Even after fifteen years, you will, at best, make three times more than your starting salary, which accounts for lifestyle inflation. By the time you finally have extra money to spend, you will either have a long list of health problems, or you will be old and gray.

Another thing that is also common in people who have poor financial skills is lifestyle inflation. You see, you might be earning $100,000 but have a very modest lifestyle. You might have a small apartment, an economy car, and perhaps a couple of hobbies. Unfortunately, if the area you are living in becomes very expensive, you can barely save any money. Let's say that you get a raise to $150,000, and you decide to celebrate. You move into a new house, you get a fancier car, your hobbies become more expensive, and you are still saving the same as you were in the beginning. Then your boss gives you another raise, and this time, you move into a new house, buy another fancy car, and buy a boat to celebrate. By the time you retire, you will have very little money to live on, and you will have to continue working until you hit the coffin. This is all too common a story, and this book aims to teach you ways to combat it.

My intention is not to give people a sure-fire way to retire early and live grand. Instead, this book is a stepping-stone for people like me, a high schooler who looks to retire early and securely. This book will show you ways to make money and to make that money work for you. One of the best quotes I have ever heard is, "If you work smart enough, you can monetize anything." This quote has stuck with me because it applies to anyone—artists selling their work, musicians doing gigs, and so many more. With financial confidence, you can do anything. As Robert Kiyosaki said in his book *Rich Dad, Poor Dad*, "Financial freedom is available to those who learn about it and work for it." And with that, let's get started.

Chapter 1: Assets and Liabilities

You might think that a well-off person would have fancy things—a Ferrari, a Louis Vuitton bag, and first-class airline tickets. The reality is that a lot of people with wealth don't flaunt it. In fact, fancy items like Gucci T-shirts and expensive cars often create an illusion of non-existent wealth. Some of the wealthiest people, like Mark Zuckerberg, Elon Musk, and Bill Gates don't wear fancy clothing or drive the most expensive cars; they live simply. In fact, there are a lot of millionaires who seem like they earn a normal amount of money because they live frugally. A rich person doesn't need to flaunt their money to gain status in society or to feel rich. This is why a lot of people with generational wealth are unknown—they simply don't spend their money conspicuously or spend it on lavish things. One of my classmates in middle school always came to school wearing simple T-shirts, jeans, and a hand-me-down hoodie. We all thought his parents didn't make much money, but it turned out that they ran one of the biggest manufacturing companies in Portland and made millions. Rich people have a secret: They acquire assets and avoid liabilities. In economics, there is a concept called the law of diminishing returns. Simply put, the law of diminishing returns states that as you get more of something, the added benefit of that extra utility decreases. For example, if you just finished a trip through a desert, the first bottle of water you drink will be amazing. The second will still feel good, but it won't give you the same amount of satisfaction as the first. Continue, and at a certain point, the water won't mean anything to you.

A common misconception is that an asset is something valuable. While this may be true, for our use case, an asset is something that pays for itself and can maintain its value. For example, a new car can lose up to 11% of its value as soon as you drive it off the lot. That means your fancy Mercedes could lose $10,000 in value the moment you leave the dealership. Unless you are collecting valuable cars, cars are not an asset as they cost you lots of money and don't make you any money at all. Even cars like a fancy BMW 7 Series rarely retain their value and often cost the owner thousands per year in maintenance.

This is why a lot of rich people buy electric cars or used cars, as they don't lose their value as fast or cost too much money in the long run. A true asset is something you own that basically pays for itself. For example, if you bought a house in 2013 for $300,000, you can now expect that house to be worth exponentially more. This means that the house has paid for itself, and now you can use it as a rental property, with the equity and the passive rental income paying for maintenance and giving you some cash in your pocket.

Meanwhile, many people assume that their primary residence is an asset, when it is actually a liability. Your house will cost money to maintain, and if you sell it, you have to find another place to live, meaning that you would have used up the money you made from selling the house, and now have to pay again for more maintenance costs, and unexpected occurrences. Rich people acquire assets as doing so allows them to make money from anywhere they please. One of the smartest people I know buys and sells houses as a real estate agent. Even though his primary residence is small, old, and not in the best part of town, he uses his real estate license to buy property for himself (making himself a nice commission) and then using it as rental property. This means that he has acquired a ton of assets, and he doesn't have very many liabilities, since he can use the rental income to pay for anything that comes his way.

Cash is known as a liquid asset because it is so easy to sell. For example, if I wanted to buy a car using a house, I would have to sell the house, get the cash, and then buy the car. In the mafia, this is known as a fence. The reason why people rob banks is that one, the money is insured, and two, since it is so easy to use cash, you don't need to find someone to sell it to. But the problem with cash is with inflation. You see, if I were on an island, and I was the only person with mangos, the mangos would be very valuable if there were lots of demand. Now let's say someone else comes to the island with mangos; now the price will drop since there is more supply and the same amount of demand. The government often has to print more money to pay for infrastructure, causing the value of money to decrease. This is why, among other reasons, the price of things like detergent has risen so much over the past few years.

Rich people know this, and they don't keep a lot of cash on hand. Many affluent people have non-liquid assets that appreciate in price; therefore, they can use the equity from those assets to pay for things. A millionaire I know has 90% of their net income in fixed assets, while the rest is in liquid assets like cash. This is why rich people don't get taxed as much. When you get a salary, the government takes its share. But if most of your money is in fixed assets, the government can't really take its share from just the value of the asset. You need to convert it into cash in order for the government to take its share. If I own a rental property worth $1 million, and it makes $10,000 a month, I can live off the $10,000 (a yearly amount of $120,000) and then use the equity of my property (which will most likely increase) as collateral for loans to buy new assets or to have in case of an emergency. This is why the British royal family is so wealthy. They own vast numbers of properties across the world (many paid for by the Crown), and then the equity and income goes to the Government or to the royals themselves. This is why you often hear on the news that billionaires pay little to nothing in taxes—they don't have that many taxable liquid assets.

On the other end of the spectrum are the liabilities. Everyone has liabilities they cannot avoid. These are things like a car, a phone, a computer, and anything else that loses its value in a short amount of time. The problem with liabilities is how easy it is to gain more of them, thinking they are assets. For example, one of my friends' parents paid $10,000 for college counseling. This counselor didn't just edit the kid's essays, he told him what activities to take, what classes to take, what exam prep to use, and controlled that kid's life for three years. In economics, there is a concept called *opportunity cost.* Opportunity cost means that when you do something, you inevitably lose something. So the goal is to reduce your opportunity cost. For this kid, his parents took on the liability of the counseling, and the kid took on the opportunity cost of not being able to enjoy his childhood and having a restricted selection of what to do in life. In the end, he went to an Ivy League school, paying $70,000 a year and was unable to find a good pathway. Since his parents paid for his counseling, he now had the liability of the college tuition, preventing him from reaching his financial goal early in life. As a high schooler, it would be easy for me to say that the opportunity of going to an Ivy League is worth the cost, but a true financial master would cringe. College is inherently an asset since it allows you to gain good job opportunities, paying for itself. However, liabilities don't have to be unpayable, they just have to suck off financial resources. This is why it is so risky to use your primary residence as an asset—it drains financial resources without providing you that much in return (in liquid assets). For our undecided scholar, he got a job after university for $90,000 a year, and he had to pay for the expense of college. I'm not saying that college is a bad investment; I am saying that you need to be careful what you consider an asset. The average person in the US has around $37,000 in student loans (Hanson,2023)[3]. This means that when they start work after graduation, they will have to spend the first six to seven years just trying to pay their loans back. If they don't, their credit score will fall, meaning that they are less likely to get housing and other types of loans. On top of that, this number doesn't even factor in graduate school, which has fewer scholarships available.

On the flip side of the coin, things that are financially considered liabilities can

---

[3] Hanson, Melanie. "Average Student Loan Debt [2023]: by Year, Age & More." *Education Data Initiative*, 22 May 2023, https://educationdata.org/average-student-loan-debt

provide a return on investment (ROI) that numbs the financial burden. A senior citizen doesn't need to pay for college or housing, so they can afford a Porsche or whatever car they desire. For them, the happiness they get from the liability offsets its financial burden. This book is not to prevent you from aspiring to expensive things. It is merely a guide for you to be able to afford those things. As my parents put it: If you want it, go work for it and get it.

One other thing to consider when you are beginning your financial journey is what assets to invest your time in. Although a cryptocurrency that gives you money might sound nice, it isn't a good use of your time, since you are not getting a good return on your investment since most of the time these schemes go bust quickly. Here is a good way to judge whether an asset is worth your time and investment: If you had only five hours in a day to gain assets, would you still consider investing your time in it? Or would you rather look for something with more value?

Just like a liability, assets can also be bad. As I mentioned before, an asset can be something that takes your time and doesn't give you much. An asset can also be something that creates a liability as a result of acquiring it. A good example is opening a business. While opening a business can provide massive amounts of profit, other assets are just liabilities dressed as assets. A good example is opening an ice cream shop in a busy part of town. Although the land and property may give you some value, the fact that you now have to run a business in a competitive part of town, vulnerable to lawsuits and legal problems, and the interest you have to pay on the store (assuming that you took out a loan to start the business) are liabilities. This "asset" proves to actually be a liability because you are sacrificing a lot in order to gain little. Make sure to value your time more than you value the asset. When you value time more than money, the money will make itself clearer. Here's a non-financial example: When I was in my sophomore year of high school, I was struggling to get an A in AP biology. I thought that the more time I invested in the class, the higher the grade I would get. I spent nights figuring out what mitochondria did and what ligase was. It consumed huge amounts of my time. When I found out that I would still get a B in the class, I realized something: Instead of focusing on my weaknesses, I should work on my strengths.

In a portfolio of stocks, it is better to cut your losses and focus on your earners. Venture capitalists use the same strategy as they invest in a business early into their creation, knowing that while most startups fail, the others will cover the losses and benefit the venture capital company.

The thing about investing is that it is impossible for all your investments to come out good. Juicero was a Silicon Valley startup that created a juice machine that squeezed juice out of pre-packaged bags of fruit. Highly successful companies like Google invested millions in the company, but an expensive product, low consumer interest, and scathing media reports caused Juicero to go bankrupt and lose most of its money in the process. Now, Google could have shut down their entire venture capital business, but they chose to go on; some of their notable investments include DocuSign, Stripe, Medium, StockX, Gitlab, and Uber. It is important for us young investors not to get discouraged after setbacks like a fallen investment. Instead, we learn from our mistakes and move on. Many successful investors have one thing in common: They hold no emotional connection to their investments. This one principle allows them to invest with a clear mind and unbiased outlook.

Likewise, like vampire assets, there are also liabilities that can turn into assets. This explains why the rich sometimes buy expensive antique cars from the early 1900s, a choice that can leave the average person scratching their head. But they are actually geniuses—they know that while the car may be liabilities for the time being, its value will increase rather than decrease, and they can later sell it for a huge profit. For example, the Tesla Roadster (The first car made by Tesla) was $100,000, and now they are going for more than double that, and collectors are actively trying to buy them. The same goes for things like Jordan Shoes, Rolex watches, fine art, fine wine, and other things that are considered rare and valuable. A good investor finds opportunities wherever they can, even if they are wrapped around liabilities.

Another thing is to hold onto your assets long enough. We all want instant gratification, but it is not always the best option. Most day traders have trouble holding onto their assets and fail to make a profit. They have to be ready to work every day the market is open and have no little job security in the event of a crash or a recession. On top of that, they also incur heavy taxes for not being able to hold on to their stocks or other assets. Investors like Warren Buffett often spend decades earning their wealth and using compound interest to be able to make billions without that much investment of their time. This is how he was able to build companies like Berkshire Hathaway while holding massive amounts of stock in Coca-Cola and Apple. Also, those who invest in good long-term assets are able to make money on the side for things like retirement or a nest egg.

There are more investment vehicles than just stocks nowadays, and in later chapters, we will go into some depth on cryptocurrencies, options, non-fungible tokens (NFTs), and other new age assets, as well as stocks and real estate. It is important not to get too far ahead of ourselves, or we will fall victim to scams, penny stocks, cryptocurrencies without any strong base, NFTs that have no value, and the thousands of vampire assets roaming the world. It is important to be able to discern between the trendsetters and the fads. Here is a list of some of the most common assets and investments.

Name	Barriers to Entry	Cost	Risk	Reputa-tion
Stocks	Few if you are over the age of 18	Varies quite heavily since shares can be either $1 or $1000	High risk because you are essentially betting on a company's performance, which is very variable	Very high since it is the backbone of Wall Street and other major financial institutions worldwide

Name	Barriers to Entry	Cost	Risk	Reputa-tion
Bonds	Few if you are over the age of 18	Varies because the price of bonds are vast	Little, since people make payments on the bonds as time goes on in increasing amounts	High since some of the biggest governments rely on bonds to get capital. Bonds are not as well known as stocks or real estate
Comm-odities	Few if you are over the age of 18	Varies because some commodities, such as gold, might be expensive whereas commodities such as oil or produce might not.	Varies because the volatility of some commodity-es can change depending on environmental or political factors.	Very high, since commodities such as gold have been used for millennia.

Chapter 1: Assets and Liabilities

Name	Barriers to Entry	Cost	Risk	Reputation
Crypto Currency	Few if you are over the age of 18	Varies because some cryptocurrencies as worth less than a penny, and others are worth thousands of dollars	Very high, since some of the most stable currencies have also been known to have sharp drops in value, and lots of cryptocurrency scams exist which can also drop the price	Low, because of the number of scams on cryptocurrency platforms, as well as the premise, which concerns governments and individual investors alike

The recent crash of FTX Trading, Ltd., a company that formerly operated a popular cryptocurrency exchange, is a good indicator of how all that glitters is not gold. The founder, Sam Bankman-Fried, also ran a company called Alameda Research, which specialized in risky cryptocurrency-based bets. Bankman-Fried ended up using clients' money to invest in Alameda, and when the crypto market crashed, all that money disappeared. He is now under arrest in the Bahamas and awaiting trial. Celebrities who endorsed FTX, including Kevin O'Leary from *Shark Tank*, are now facing PR disasters.

But there are companies that invest in assets and liabilities on a daily basis. Working in these companies can be extremely lucrative. Some of the most popular ones are hedge fund, mutual fund, venture capitalists, and angel investing firms.

Hedge funds are actively managed investment pools, with managers who use a variety of strategies to give their clients a better return. One of the main things that set hedge funds apart is that they are not regulated by the Securities and Exchange Commission (SEC), and they cannot take money from the public. This is why most hedge funds are not known to the public or are household names. Clients of hedge funds are typically high-net-worth individuals or groups. Hedge funds are known to use more risky methods of investing, such as leveraging. Hedge funds also usually charge a 1-2% fee of the assets, and a 20% performance fee. The main reason why hedge funds are popular in the world of finance is their potential to beat mutual funds. Throughout the early 1960s, hedge funds dramatically outperformed the market while still being relatively unknown to the public. These funds focused on stock picking, hedging, and long-term leveraging, allowing the fund's investors to make massive returns compared to the aforementioned mutual funds. This was until the bear market of 1973-74, when multiple big hedge fund groups went out of business. Hedge funds made a return in the late 1980s, but then many of them, too, fell victim to the dot-com bubble, the 2008 financial crisis, and other market drops. The main reason why many hedge funds went bankrupt during the dot-com bubble was because they used leverage as well as betting on companies with seemingly no value, inflating the stock price until it burst. In 2019, hedge funds managed $3.6 trillion in assets. Most hedge funds only accept individuals with an annual income over $200,000 or $1 million in assets (excluding primary residence) although some have higher minimums. Since hedge funds are not regulated by the SEC, they can invest in multiple areas such as real estate, land, currency, derivatives, and commodities.

If you would rather work with a group of investors, mutual funds comprise a pool of money collected from many investors. These funds are used to purchase a variety of investments to remain diversified: stocks, bonds, and other assets. They are managed by money managers and, compared to hedge funds, they are more highly regulated and can offer somewhat less risk. Mutual funds give small or individual investors access to professionally managed portfolios of equities, bonds, and other securities. Each shareholder, therefore, participates proportionally in the gains or losses of the fund. Mutual funds use money from investors to buy securities, such as bonds or stocks. The price of a mutual fund is referred to as the net asset value (NAV). This is derived by dividing the total value of the securities in the portfolio by the total amount of shares outstanding. Most mutual funds hold over 100 different securities, meaning that the investors can get lots of diversification at a low price. Income can be earned from stock dividends, if the fund holds securities that pay them. If the fund's holdings increase in value, and the manager decides to sell them, then the fund generates capital gains. Mutual funds are usually managed by a corporate entity such as Vanguard or Fidelity. Equity funds invest mainly in stocks and can invest in small or large cap companies. Fixed-income funds invest mainly in securities that have a fixed rate of return, such as government bonds, corporate bonds, or debt instruments. Index funds buy stocks that correspond with a major market index, like the S&P 500. Balanced funds invest in a variety of investments and cater to the individual investor. Money market funds are very safe investments that consist mainly of government treasury bills. Income funds give investors a steady rate of income, and deal primarily with bonds. Lastly, ETFs employ strategies consistent with mutual funds, but they are structured as investment trusts that are traded on stock exchanges and have the added benefits of stocks. This means that they can be bought at any time during trading hours and can be sold short or on margin. Mutual funds typically have a 1-3% fee, but many have higher fees and a lack of transparency in the holdings. They are not FDIC insured and often have a large cash presence in their portfolios. This means that you might be more vulnerable to unexpected inflation due to the large cash holding.

Venture capitalists are similar to angel investors with one main difference—venture capitalists are employees of another company that pools funds from other investors. Another big difference is that unlike angel investors, they usually help businesses when they are ready to commercialize and then cash out when the business has grown. Venture capitalists are willing to risk their investments in companies because they hope they will get cash payouts if the company succeeds. Unfortunately, this is a risky endeavor, since the businesses they invest in are startups and can easily fail. Wealthy individuals, insurance companies, pension funds, foundations, and corporate pension funds may pool money together into a fund to be controlled by a VC firm. All partners have part ownership of the fund, but it is the VC firm that controls where the fund is invested, usually in businesses or ventures that most banks or capital markets would consider too risky for investment.

Angel investing is when a person with a high net worth decides to invest in small startup businesses or entrepreneurs. Usually, in exchange for cash, they gain some equity or ownership in the company. One of the most publicized versions of angel investing is the TV show *Shark Tank.* In this show, billionaires invest in small startup companies and make "sharky" investments in the business. Because the nature of angel investing is risky, most investors only allocate 10% of their portfolio to angel investing; it is a way to invest excess funds. Some angel investors create a pool of funds, which they then invest in the business. The main difference between angel investing and crowdfunding is that angel investing is usually a smaller group of individuals funding a business; crowdfunding is a large group of over twenty individuals investing in a venture in exchange for the company's product rather than ownership. Angel investors are normally individuals who have gained "accredited" status, but this isn't a prerequisite. The SEC defines an "accredited investor" as one with a net worth of $1 million in assets or more (excluding personal residences), or having earned $200,000 in income for the previous two years, or having a combined income of $300,000 for married couples.

Another asset that people have been investing in since the dawn of time is gold. It is not just gold, in fact, but also silver, copper, and platinum. Precious metal investors may not make the most gains, but there is a massive reason why they still invest in them—consistency.

The history of investing in gold dates back thousands of years, making it one of the oldest forms of investment known to humanity. Gold has always been revered for its rarity, beauty, and intrinsic value, making it a store of wealth and a symbol of power and prestige in many civilizations.

Ancient civilizations such as the Egyptians, Greeks, and Romans recognized the value of gold and used it as a medium of exchange, a unit of accounting, and a store of value. The Silk Road, which connected Europe, Asia, and Africa, facilitated the flow of gold across different regions, promoting its use as a global currency.

During the Middle Ages, gold was associated with religious significance, with many religious institutions accumulating vast amounts of it in the form of jewelry, ornaments, and religious artifacts.

In the 19th century, the gold rush in various parts of the world, such as California, Australia, and South Africa, led to significant increases in the global supply of gold. This, in turn, influenced the establishment of gold standards in different economies, where the value of the currency was pegged to a specific amount of gold. The gold standard system was widely adopted until the mid-20th century, when most countries switched to fiat currencies.

In the 20th century, geopolitical uncertainties, economic crises, and inflationary pressures led to increased demand for gold as a safe-haven asset. The United States' abandonment of the gold standard in 1971 further contributed to gold's appeal as a hedge against currency depreciation and economic instability.

Today, gold continues to be a popular investment option due to its status as a tangible asset with intrinsic value and limited supply. Investors use gold to diversify their portfolios and protect against inflation, economic downturns, and currency devaluation.

If you are interested in getting into the action, then here are some strategies to invest in this metal.

1. Physical gold: This involves buying gold in the form of gold bars, coins, or jewelry. Owning physical gold allows investors to have direct ownership and control over their assets. However, storage and security can be concerns, and additional costs may be associated with purchasing and storing physical gold.

2. Gold exchange-traded funds (ETFs): Gold ETFs are investment funds that hold gold assets and trade on stock exchanges like regular stocks. Investing in gold through ETFs offers liquidity and ease of trading, and it eliminates the need for physical storage. It is a popular choice for investors who want exposure to the precious metal without owning physical gold.

3. Gold mining stocks: Investing in gold mining companies provides exposure to the gold market without directly owning physical

gold. The performance of these stocks is influenced not only by the price of gold but also by the company's financial health, production efficiency, and management decisions.

4. Gold futures and options: These are derivative financial instruments that allow investors to speculate on the future price of gold without owning the physical metal. Futures and options trading can be more complex and risky compared to other methods of investing in gold, and it's generally more suitable for experienced investors.

5. Gold accumulation plans: Some financial institutions offer gold accumulation plans, where investors can regularly contribute funds to accumulate gold over time. These plans can be an affordable way to invest in gold incrementally.

6. Gold certificates: Gold certificates represent ownership of a certain quantity of gold held by a financial institution or a custodian. Investors can buy and sell these

certificates without physically handling the gold.

With a basic understanding of assets and liabilities, you are already on the right track to becoming a successful investor. Acquiring assets is one of the best ways to create generational wealth because you can always pass down good assets to your family, creating a financial safety net for them. Many people have heard of the curse, whereby the first generation will work hard to create their wealth, the second generation will see how hard the first generation worked and will grow the wealth, and the third generation will lose the wealth because they don't know the value of the money they have in their hands. Even for wealthy families, learning the difference between assets and liabilities is the first step in securing their wealth for many more future generations.

Chapter 2: Wolf of Personal Finance Avenue

If you're like me, you've probably heard about the film *The Wolf of Wall Street* featuring Leonardo Di Caprio and portraying the life and trials of prolific stock jockey Jordan Belfort. In the movie, the lavish life of people working in finance fascinated me, and one line in particular struck me, "I want you to deal with your problems by becoming rich!" This line stuck out to me because it made me think how many of our problems in life are attributed to finance. For example, most people go to school to get into a good college; they go to a good college to get a good job, and they get a good job to be able to make money. Any person will tell you that it is not efficient, but it is safe. Like I mentioned, college costs an average of $35,000 in the US per year, meaning that you will spend the first ten years of your professional career just trying to pay back your student loans before being able to think about buying a home or starting a family. Even as a high schooler, it stuns me that some people are willing to go to school for twelve years to earn the same amount as someone who worked for those twelve years. Or, you can do both through the power of stocks and compound interest.

Stocks are just a fancy way of saying that you own a share of a company. For example, if I own a share of Apple, it means that I own a very miniscule part of Apple. And when I sell the stock, I sell it to another investor and not back to Apple. When I sell the stock, I get back what the company's share is worth now. If one share of a company was worth $12 when I bought it and was worth $14 when I sold it, that means the value of the company has increased. So, the entire point of stock trading is to be able to gauge whether a company will increase in value or not. Unfortunately, it is highly volatile.

For example, electric car company Rivian was riding on a stock high thanks to its contract with Amazon to make electric delivery vehicles. This increased the value of the company in the eyes of investors and allowed the stock to gain tons of value on its initial public offering (IPO). An IPO is when a stock is first available to be bought by the public. A company sells shares in order to raise capital. A company must own at least

50% of its stock to be able to make any major decisions (by internal board or owner), and most companies can afford to lose some of their ownership to raise some cash. Back to our example, Rivian then lost the contract, and the stock has been falling since. It is important not to board the hype train and fail to see the bigger picture.

In another example, remember Kanye West? Before all the controversy surrounding him, he was one of the most coveted figures in the sneaker world. His Yeezy shoes were at one point more popular than the Air Jordan 1s, and it seemed like Adidas and Kanye would go to the moon. Unfortunately, the hype train ended. With a few lackluster releases and the feeling of exclusivity gone, the Yeezy brand started to die, and as a result, Nike's strategy of artificial demand proved to come out on top. The fact is that stocks are very volatile, and a true investor needs to decide whether they will play the long or short game.

During the bull market of late 2020 and mid-2021, the idea of fast money seemed to be everywhere. And in fact many people (including me) were drawn into the hype and thought the market would continue to rise for the foreseeable future. This led many to buy into crypto with less than reputable bases. These so-called "investors" ended up seeing their entire portfolios go into the red and losing their Lamborghinis and Rolex watches. A true investor first gains an immense amount of knowledge before making decisions like putting all their money on a cryptocurrency promoted by someone with no investing knowledge.

Stocks are good investments because of the amount of information available to the public about how to invest. You can be a casual investor and trade using an app on your phone, or you can be a hardcore day trader and use complex software that allows you to make split-second decisions about the right time to buy and sell. Also, unlike real estate, the taxes on stocks are usually pretty minimal. You usually pay a fee to buy the stock through your broker. When you sell your stock, the government usually takes a tax on the return you made. But luckily, a lot of brokers now make it much easier to buy and sell through strategies like no commissions or no trading fees. Also, the longer you hold onto your stocks, the less tax you have to pay when you end up selling them.

One of the best things about stocks is that you don't even have to pick them individually—you can invest in them through ETFs and index funds. Simply put, an index fund is a group of stocks that a company has picked and that you, the buyer, can buy a share of. This relieves you of the hassle of trying to diversify your portfolio yourself, and when you sell the stock, the issuer of the index fund takes only a small amount, leaving you with most of the profits. This means that you have to hold on to your shares until you need the money, and then you can reap the profits. Another cool thing about index funds is that they remain relatively stable during times of financial unrest. This means that even during a recession, you can count on the people running the fund to be able to give you money after the recession ends. ETFs are very similar to index funds, but have a few key differences. For one, shares of ETFs are traded like individual stocks rather than shares of the fund. Another thing to note is that an ETF is being traded by a group of people. A good way to put this is if you and your friends decided to start a laundromat, you would all pitch in and work to make sure that you gain a profit. On the other hand, an index fund is like just taking the profits from the laundromat. Both long-term investing methods are good for people who don't have the time or energy to invest in individual stocks. Also, many companies also pay out dividends to their shareholders. A dividend payment is a company giving its investors a share of its profits. Usually, it's a very low amount, but over time, you can easily make a decent amount of money just from the dividend payments. This is how many people are able to retire early—they get dividend payments regularly, allowing them to be able to sustain themselves and beat inflation.

The best thing about stocks is that you are actively investing in the company. This is why many banks have started impact portfolios, investing your money into companies that do good for the world. Other investment classes don't have this type of flexibility, meaning that if you really love a company, they would appreciate it if you invested in them. Stocks are also a great way for teenagers to learn how to invest because they are simple to trade and don't require too much technical knowledge to get started.

Investing apps have become so simple to use that you can start investing in a matter of minutes. On top of that, stock investing is a good platform to learn technical analysis and other forms of data analysis that you can apply to other investments as well. Some of the most powerful investing firms in the world use stocks as a good way of giving returns to their customers.

Stocks are typically not as volatile as something like options or foreign exchange (Forex) trading because of their long-run nature. Even though you are not likely old enough to think about retirement, stock trading through things like index funds and ETFs are good ways to get started. Stocks are also preferred because people can pick and choose what companies they want to invest in and whether they want to trust them with their money. Companies also have to present a lot of their financials to investors, making it easy for investors to gauge the company's strength.

It is a common misconception that people under the age of eighteen cannot invest in stocks. If you are a minor, you can invest through a custodial account or through a mutual fund. Another easier way is to find an investing app that is focused on teenage investing. These apps will allow you to invest through your parents' bank account. This means that your parents can also control your investments as well. If you start early, you will be able to benefit from compound earnings, so by the time you graduate college or need money for other reasons, you will have it.

Stocks are also a good way of learning financial principles such as saving and budgeting. A good rule is to spend only the gains you make on the investments. If you by chance need the money urgently, you can still withdraw all your money—just make sure that you can afford it. A big mistake that many people make is not waiting long enough before they sell their stocks. This will cause them to get taxed more, lose out on possible future gains, and miss out on the compound earnings. So, if you are not desperate to get the money now, wait as long as possible before you sell your stocks.

Investing in the stock market can be a great way to grow your wealth over the long term. However, it is important to approach investing with a sound strategy in order to maximize your chances of success. Here are a few key strategies that can help you make good investment decisions in the stock market:

1. Diversification: One of the most important principles of investing is diversification, which means spreading your investments across a variety of different assets. This helps to minimize risk, as it ensures that you are not overly reliant on any one particular investment. For example, you could diversify by investing in a mix of stocks, bonds, and cash, as well as in different sectors and industries.

2. Long-term perspective: Successful investors tend to take a long-term perspective when it comes to their investments. This means focusing on the long-term growth potential of an investment, rather than trying to chase short-term gains. By holding onto your investments for the long term, you can ride out market fluctuations and give your investments time to grow.

3. Fundamental analysis: Another important strategy is to conduct a thorough fundamental analysis of a company before investing in its stock. This involves evaluating the company's financial health, competitive advantage, management, and other factors that can affect its long-term prospects. By understanding the underlying fundamentals of a company, you can make more informed decisions about whether to invest.

4. Risk management: It is also important to have a risk management strategy in place to help protect your investments from potential losses. This can involve setting stop-loss orders to limit your potential losses, diversifying your portfolio, and keeping a portion of your investments in cash or other low-risk assets.

5. Regular rebalancing: As your investments grow and change in value over time, it is important to regularly review and rebalance your portfolio to ensure that it remains in line with your

investment goals and risk tolerance. This can involve selling off assets that have become overvalued and purchasing undervalued assets to help maintain a balanced portfolio.

By following these strategies, you can increase your chances of success in the stock market and potentially achieve long-term growth for your investments. It is important to keep in mind, however, that investing in the stock market carries some level of risk, and it is important to be prepared for market fluctuations and unexpected events. As with any investment, it is important to carefully consider your own financial situation and risk tolerance before making any investment decisions.

If you are willing to take on more risk, options trading is also an interesting opportunity. Options are a type of financial derivative; you can buy or sell the right to buy or sell an underlying asset at a specific price (called the "strike price") on or before a specific date (called the "expiration date"). Options can be used as a hedge against market volatility, to generate income, or to speculate on price movements of an underlying asset. There are two types of options: call options and put options. A call option gives you the right, but not the obligation, to buy the underlying asset at the strike price. A put option gives you the right, but not the obligation, to sell the underlying asset at the strike price. The price of an option is determined by several factors, including the price of the underlying asset, the strike price, the expiration date, and the volatility of the underlying asset. The price of an option is also influenced by supply and demand in the options market. Options trading can be complex and carries a high level of risk, so it is important to thoroughly understand the mechanics of options and to carefully consider your investment objectives, risk tolerance, and financial situation before getting involved. It is also important to work with a broker or financial advisor who is knowledgeable about options and can help you make informed decisions.

If options trading is a bit too complex and risky for you, then short selling is another investing strategy that can give significant returns in a short amount of time. Short selling is a trading strategy that involves selling securities that the seller does not own in the hopes of buying them back at a lower price in the future. It is a way for investors to bet against a particular stock or the market as a whole. In the stock market, short selling can be a risky but potentially profitable strategy, and it has both pros and cons.

One of the main advantages of short selling is that it allows investors to profit from declining market conditions. If an investor believes that a particular stock or the market as a whole is overvalued, they can sell the stock short and profit if the price falls. This can be particularly useful in times of market instability or economic downturn, as investors can use short selling to hedge against potential losses in their portfolio. By selling a stock short, an investor can profit from a decline in the stock's price, even if the overall market is going down. This can be a useful tool for investors looking to diversify their portfolio and reduce risk. A lot of successful financial firms used short selling during the 2008 financial recession to make their positions very strong when the market would, theoretically, recover.

However, short selling also has its downsides. One of the main risks is the potential for losses. When an investor sells a stock short, they are essentially borrowing the stock from someone else and agreeing to pay back the loan at a later date. If the price of the stock goes up instead of down, the investor will have to buy it back at a higher price, resulting in a loss. There is no upper limit to these losses, as the price of the stock could theoretically keep going up indefinitely.

Another risk of short selling is the potential for a short squeeze. A short squeeze occurs when a stock's price starts to rise rapidly, causing short sellers to panic and buy back the stock to cover their positions. This can lead to a further increase in the stock's price, causing even more short sellers to cover their positions, and so on. This can result in significant losses for short sellers, as they are forced to buy back the stock at increasingly high prices.

Short selling is not without controversy. Some critics argue that it can contribute to market manipulation and instability, as short sellers may spread negative information about a company in an attempt to drive down its stock price. This can lead to a negative feedback loop, the negative sentiment driving the price down further, which may in turn attract more short sellers, and so on.

Overall, short selling can be a useful tool for investors looking to profit from declining market conditions or to hedge against potential losses. However, it is also a risky strategy that can result in heavy losses and may contribute to market manipulation and instability. As with any investment strategy, it is important for investors to carefully consider the potential risks and rewards before deciding to engage in short selling.

Since options trading is super risky, it is important to practice first before starting to trade. You should seriously consider investing in options only if you are willing to take on the risk and commit the time. Also, there are no real investing platforms for teenagers to invest in options. Therefore, you need to be ready to learn a lot of concepts well beyond the scope of this book. Another problem with options trading is that you have to spend quite a bit of time on it, so unless you are prepared to make the time commitment, it's best to avoid it.

Successful billionaires like Warren Buffett use a strategy that gains money over a long period of time. They invest for the long run. You see, there is a concept in economics that was coined by Albert Einstein known as compound interest. Basically, it allows you to calculate how much you will make based on the return a certain product or service provides. For example, let's say I make 7% return on an investment each year, that amount will compound and the next year, I'll make a 14% return on that original investment. As time goes on, you will start to make more and more money, and before you know it, you will have a source of passive income to support yourself on. Even if the market might not seem good to invest in, the beauty of compound interest is that you don't need to play the short game. For example, one of our family friends has a massive house, nestled on top of a hill, with balconies and other luxury amenities. Their only income comes from their hotel. The trick is that they bought the place during the 2008 financial crisis when the price of homes plummeted, and that allowed them to buy it at a very low price. Now on Zillow, the house is worth at least $2 million, and they paid a quarter of that. They were able to foresee the value of their home exponentially increasing, yielding them a high capital gain, and were able to use the equity in their home to re-invest into other assets. In fact, many people I know have struck it rich, investing when the market was at rock bottom and waiting ten years to be able to realize the gains and as a result, retire.

Chapter 2: Wolf of Personal Finance Avenue

Chapter 3: Real Estate Boogaloo

Real estate is one of the most powerful investment classes available. In fact, 80% of Americans become millionaires through real estate (Eilish, 2022)[4]. Real estate in a geographically large country like the US allows for cheaper land prices and more availability. During the pandemic, housing prices started to skyrocket, which meant that people who had just starter homes were seeing their homes' value double or even triple. A simple search on houses near your area will reveal just how lucrative real estate can be. As a high schooler, you probably don't have hundreds of thousands of dollars at your disposal, but you can start to learn the foundations of how to invest, buy, sell, and house hack.

Real estate refers to the ownership, use, and development of land, as well as any buildings or structures on it. It includes a wide range of assets, including residential properties, commercial properties, and

[4] Kelly, Jack. "." . - *YouTube*, 2 October 2022, https://www.forbes.com/sites/jackkelly/2023/05/23/the-making-of-a-millionaire-and-why-100k-is-no-longer-the-benchmark-salary-for-wealth-in-america/?sh=61e7e0c2af28 .

industrial properties. Real estate can be owned by individuals, a group of investors, businesses, or governments, and it can be used for a variety of purposes, including living, working, and investing. The value of real estate is often influenced by a variety of factors, including location, size, condition, inflation of building costs, and demand. Since the value of real estate doesn't typically change too rapidly, it is a good long-term investment. Also, many people don't just acquire real estate to invest in, they house hack.

The concept of house hacking is very simple: finding ways to pay as little as possible for living expenses in both urban and suburban areas. People buy a townhouse or a duplex; they own both units, living in one and renting out the other. This means that their tenant covers their living costs as well as providing positive cash flow in many cases. Another method of house hacking is if you run your own business. In a lot of states, you can get a tax break when you run your business from home; you can write off some of the costs of that home on your taxes. If you have a secondary residence that you don't use all the time, then you can easily rent it out on Zillow, Airbnb, or other rental platforms.

You are probably reading this and wondering how you will ever be able to afford such big expenses, but there is a way to essentially get a discount on these properties. When you turn eighteen, you can take a test that allows you to become a real estate agent, meaning that you will get a commission on any house you buy, since you sold it to yourself. Therefore, your commission can act as a discount or just extra money in the bank. Therefore, when you are sixteen or seventeen, you can start to prepare for the exam and take it as soon as you turn eighteen. This will not only look good on your résumé, but it will also give you a source of income. Having a real estate license can come in handy when you are trying to explain to colleges your commitment to the field of business and investing. The license will also allow you to network with other agents, meaning that their experience can influence your decisions in the field.

With housing prices skyrocketing, realizing a discount with commissions on property purchases is very helpful. Getting your real estate license is an easy way for you as a high schooler to learn not only the ins and outs of real estate, but a lot of the topics you learn while studying for the exam can help you better understand other investing concepts.

Learning about real estate is also a good way of figuring out what types of assets make money and what don't. A lot of us have seen home renovation shows about people who buy run-down houses and renovate them. In these shows, there's a term a lot of people use: equity. Equity is the amount of money you would get if you decided to liquidate, or sell, an asset. So, while you might think that people buying "fixer-uppers" is a stupid idea, in reality, they are just building up the equity of a home and then selling it at a profit. Think about it this way. Let's say you just got your dad's old bike, and it is in awful shape. The first thing you do is clean it up and fix anything that is broken. Then you sell the bike for a larger amount than you paid for it. People use this same concept to buy properties that are otherwise overlooked.

After the 2008 financial recession, many prospective real estate investors began looking into bank foreclosures. You see, during the recession, many people took out loans for houses and could not pay them back. When they had to pay their loans, they were forced to sell their properties, or worse, the bank seized their properties in order to recover the money. This created an influx of cheap family homes that the banks were trying to get rid of as fast as possible, meaning they were selling them at a loss. People bought these super cheap homes, put in a little bit of renovation, and then sold them for a massive profit once the housing market started to rise. To this day, you can go to Zillow and look at the prices of houses and see the sharp drop and the steady increase. Just like Newton said, what goes up must come down, so a good investor always finds a way to make profits even when the market is going down. This is why it is always important to save your money, so when the market goes down, the question will be, how can I get more money to invest? and not, how can I get more money to pay for rent? It is a good practice to have enough money saved so you can pay your expenses for at least three months.

Chapter 3: Real Estate Boogaloo

Real estate is also one of the most lucrative ways to make passive income. Because people always need houses to live in, you can buy rental properties to gain some passive income. Earlier in the chapter, I talked about house hacking, and I mentioned how to live in one unit of a house and rent out the other. While this may be good if you can handle only one property, the real money comes when you can rent out houses. This is probably one of the easier investment concepts to explain. You first buy a rental property in a good location where people are willing to live. This is important because you don't want to buy a house in the middle of nowhere and expect people to come and live there. Next, you do any necessary renovations to the house. This builds the house's equity and makes it more attractive to people wanting to rent it out. The last step is the most complicated one: listing the property. There are many ways to do this, such as hiring a real estate agent to list the property. This is expensive, but a realtor will likely know the best ways to get interest in your property. The second method is to hire a company like Zeus to rent the house for you. These companies pay rent for your property. They then allow companies' employees to stay there. The companies usually cover most of the utility bills and maintenance fees, but it is hard to get a house listed on these websites. The last method is to list the house yourself. This is the riskiest option, but it is the cheapest, and you end up getting to keep more of the profits. If your house stays in good condition, then you are basically getting an extra paycheck every month without having to spend lots of time. This is one of the biggest reasons why real estate accounts for 80% of the wealth in the United States—real estate is simply one of the biggest and most powerful asset classes to exist. While the stock market is risky and will get you average returns, real estate is not as risky but has large returns when you do it properly.

But even real estate has some downsides, as we saw in the 2008 market crash. The 2008 financial crisis, also known as the global financial crisis or the Great Recession, was a severe worldwide economic downturn that began in 2007 and lasted until around 2009. It was caused by a number of factors, including the bursting of a housing bubble, the proliferation of risky mortgage products, and the failures of large financial institutions. The housing bubble was fueled by the easy availability of mortgage credit, which led to a significant increase in the value of real estate. Many people were able to take out mortgages to buy homes, even if they couldn't afford them, because the banks believed that the value of the homes would continue to rise. However, when the bubble eventually burst, the value of these homes plummeted, leaving many homeowners with properties that were worth much less than the amount they owed on their mortgages. This led to a wave of foreclosures, as people were unable to make their mortgage payments. The crisis also had a major impact on the real estate market. As the value of homes declined, the demand for real estate fell, leading to a drop in prices. This, in turn, made it difficult for homeowners to sell their properties, as they were often worth less than what was owed on them. The crisis also made it harder for people to get mortgages, as banks became more cautious about lending money.

However, this book is not a cautionary tale; it is a way for you to avoid the same mistakes that others have made. So, here are some investing strategies that you can use for real estate investing in the future.

1. Diversify your portfolio: It is important to diversify your real estate portfolio by investing in

different types of properties, such as residential, commercial, and industrial. This can help to spread risk and increase the chances of success.

2. Understand the local market: It is crucial to have a deep understanding of the local real estate market in order to make informed investment decisions. This includes understanding factors such as demand for rental properties, median home prices, and potential for price appreciation.

3. Research potential investment properties: Before making any investment, it is important to thoroughly research the property in question. This includes reviewing the property's condition, location, and potential for future appreciation.

4. Consider the tax implications: Investing in real estate can have significant tax implications, so it is important to understand the tax laws that apply to your investments. This includes understanding the tax consequences of different types of

real estate investments, such as owning a rental property or flipping a house.

5. Develop a long-term plan: Real estate investing is a long-term game, so it is important to have a clear plan in place for the long haul. This includes setting goals, creating a budget, and developing a plan for managing and maintaining your properties.

6. Consider working with a real estate professional: If you are new to real estate investing, it may be helpful to work with a real estate professional to guide you through the process. This could include a real estate agent, property manager, or financial advisor.

7. Utilize leverage: One way to potentially increase your return on investment in real estate is to utilize leverage, such as taking out a mortgage to purchase a property. Just be sure to carefully consider the risks and benefits of leveraging your investments.

8. Stay up to date: The real estate market is constantly changing, so it is important to stay up to date on market trends and

developments. This includes keeping track of economic indicators, such as interest rates and employment data, as well as monitoring local market conditions.

By following these strategies, you can increase your chances of success as a real estate investor and potentially achieve your financial goals. However, it is important to keep in mind that investing in real estate carries inherent risks, and it is always wise to thoroughly research and carefully consider any investment before committing your money.

Lastly, real estate can be used for more than just renting out properties. For one, you can sublet properties. Let me give you a scenario. Perhaps because of problems in a different part of the country, you have to leave your rented apartment to go and help. Since you don't want your apartment to just gather dust, you can sublet it. You rent from your landlord, and then you rent to someone else (a subtenant). You can charge the subtenant more than what your landlord charges you, meaning that it is a win-win scenario for both people. Many college students sublet their apartments while they go back home for vacation or if they decide to move to a different apartment. Make sure your landlord is okay with you subletting your home; it's illegal to sublet without the landlord's permission.

Let's say in the future, your parents give you their vacation home or a farm property that you have no interest in living in. The problem is, you don't have the time to rent out the property, meaning that you are losing money. An easy solution is to list your spare property on Airbnb or a similar website to allow people to stay there while you make profit. Many people buy homes just to rent them out on Airbnb. This is why a lot of vacation towns had a massive surge in real estate prices after the popularization of holiday rental platforms. Good opportunities are always available; it is up to us young investors to grab them and seize the moment.

Obtaining a real estate license can be a great opportunity for you to learn valuable skills and potentially start a rewarding career in the real estate industry. However, preparing for the real estate license exam can be a daunting task, as it requires a significant amount of knowledge and dedication. Here are some tips for you to prepare:

1. Understand the requirements: Different states have different requirements for obtaining a real estate license. Make sure to familiarize yourself with the requirements in your state, such as the age and educational requirements and any other necessary prerequisites.

2. Enroll in a real estate pre-licensing course: Many states require applicants to complete a certain number of hours of real estate education before they can take the license exam. Enrolling in a pre-licensing course can provide you with a solid foundation of knowledge and help you prepare for the exam.

3. Study and practice: The real estate license exam covers a wide range of topics, including real estate law, property ownership, and real estate math. To ensure that you are fully prepared, it is

important to study and practice as much as possible. Consider purchasing study materials, such as practice exams and flashcards, and set aside dedicated time each day to review the material.

4. Take advantage of online resources: There are many online resources available to help you prepare for the real estate license exam. Consider joining online study groups or taking online practice exams to test your knowledge and identify areas where you need to improve.

5. Find a mentor: A mentor in the real estate industry can be a valuable resource as you prepare for the license exam, providing guidance, advice, and support as you navigate the process of becoming a licensed real estate agent.

6. Stay organized: It can be easy to get overwhelmed as you prepare for the license exam, so it is important to stay organized and manage your time effectively. Consider creating a study schedule and breaking it down into manageable chunks. This can

help you stay on track and ensure that you are making progress towards your goal of becoming a licensed real estate agent.

By following these tips, you can set yourself up for success as you prepare for the exam. While the process may be challenging, the reward of becoming a licensed real estate agent can be well worth the effort. A lot of people who have their licenses aren't even realtors themselves but rather property investors.

Chapter 4: Bonding with Bonds!

Bonds are a type of investment that allows organizations to borrow money from investors. When you buy a bond, you are essentially lending money to the issuer, who agrees to pay you back the principal (the amount of money you lent) plus interest at a later date. Bonds are typically issued by governments, municipalities, and corporations, and they are used to finance a variety of projects, such as building infrastructure, funding research and development, or expanding a business.

There are several different types of bonds, each with its own set of characteristics and risks. Some of the most common types of bonds include:

1. Treasury bonds: These are bonds issued by the federal government to finance its operations and debt. They are some of the safest investments because they are backed by the full faith and credit of the United States government.
2. Municipal bonds: These are bonds issued by cities, states, and other

local governments to fund a variety of projects, such as schools, roads, and other infrastructure. Municipal bonds are generally considered to be safe investments because they are backed by the taxing power of the issuer.

3. Corporate bonds: These are bonds issued by companies to raise capital for a variety of purposes, such as expanding their operations or funding research and development. Corporate bonds carry more risk than Treasury or municipal bonds because they are not backed by the government, and the issuer's ability to make interest and principal payments may be impacted by the company's financial health.

4. High-yield bonds: Also known as junk bonds, these are bonds issued by companies that have a lower credit rating and are considered riskier than investment-grade bonds. While they may offer a higher interest rate to compensate for the added risk, there is a higher likelihood

that the issuer might default on the payments.

When you buy a bond, you agree to lend a certain amount of money to the issuer for a set period of time, known as the term or maturity of the bond. The issuer agrees to pay you a fixed amount of interest on the bond, known as the coupon rate, until the bond matures. At the end of the term, the issuer will pay back the principal to the bondholder.

The value of a bond can fluctuate based on a variety of factors, including changes in interest rates, the creditworthiness of the issuer, and the overall state of the economy. When interest rates rise, the value of existing bonds tends to fall, because new bonds being issued will have higher interest rates and may be more attractive to investors. Conversely, when interest rates fall, the value of existing bonds tends to rise because they offer a higher yield than new bonds.

Bonds can be a useful investment for people who are looking to diversify their portfolio and potentially earn a steady stream of income. However, it is important to carefully consider the risks associated with bonds and to choose investments that align with your financial goals and risk tolerance. It is also a good idea to work with a financial advisor or professional to help you understand the different types of bonds and determine which ones may be suitable for your needs. Now, a high-end financial advisor will most likely not cater to the needs of teenagers, so it is a good idea to wait a bit before you start to invest in bonds.

There is another alternative to bonds if you want something more stable for things like retirement—annuities. The easiest way to describe an annuity is that it gives you a fixed amount of income throughout the entire investment period. This means that if you invest $100 into an annuity, and it promises you a 5% return each year for five years, you will get the 5% regardless of market conditions. Many annuities also come with protections to safeguard your principal, so if your investment is under a certain amount, the bank will maintain your principle at the same level. You might think that this allows younger investors to invest and have a safe source of income, but there are a few catches. For one, annuities don't pay out a lot in interest, meaning that a lot of the time you might only be able to barely beat inflation. Another thing to consider is that there is a surrender period, which means you cannot make withdrawals from your annuity within a certain timeframe. You may have to pay fees if you withdraw more than a certain amount from your account. There are also fees that may cut into your overall earnings besides the one I just mentioned. Another problem is that in order to invest in the annuity, you need a lump sum of money, which you may not have. This makes it less accessible than the stock market, which has lower barriers to entry.

While bonds and annuities don't get the same type of exposure that other asset classes do, they really are some of the most powerful tools for retirement. As a teenager, you are probably not worrying too much about retirement. As you are young and can afford more risk, it is generally agreed that you should invest in stocks and real estate. This is because the chances of making more money in the long run are higher. Once you are settled down and ready to prepare for retirement, you can start investing in bonds to make sure you have a good retirement fund. Also, bonds are reasonably strong against inflation. This means that even during high inflation, as we saw in 2020, bonds still fared reasonably well and provided investors with returns that beat inflation.

Chapter 5: Cryptocurrency Frenzy

C ryptocurrency is a type of digital or virtual currency that uses cryptography for security and is not backed by any government or central bank. Cryptocurrencies are decentralized systems that allow for the creation, transfer, and verification of transactions using a secure network of computers called nodes. The best-known cryptocurrency is Bitcoin, but there are many others, such as Ethereum, Litecoin, and Dogecoin.

One of the main benefits of cryptocurrency is that it allows for fast and secure peer-to-peer transactions without the need for a third party, such as a bank or credit card company. This means that users can send and receive payments instantly, anywhere in the world, without the need for high fees or long wait times.

Another advantage of cryptocurrency is that it is decentralized, meaning that it is not controlled by any single authority or organization. This makes it resistant to censorship and allows for more freedom and privacy in financial transactions.

Cryptocurrencies have the potential to revolutionize the way we think about money and financial systems. Because they are not tied to any specific country or economy, they could potentially be used to store value and make transactions in a more stable and secure way. You see, cryptocurrency is stored on the blockchain. The blockchain is a decentralized digital ledger that records transactions across a network of computers. It allows for the creation of secure and transparent record-keeping systems without the need for a central authority. This technology is the backbone of cryptocurrencies such as Bitcoin and Ethereum, and it has the potential to revolutionize a wide range of industries, from finance and healthcare to supply-chain management and voting systems. At its core, a blockchain is a growing list of records called blocks, which are linked and secured using cryptography. Each block contains a cryptographic hash of the previous block, a timestamp, and transaction data. This design ensures that once a block is added to the chain, it cannot be altered or deleted. To understand how blockchain technology affects cryptocurrency, it's important to first understand how traditional currencies work. Most currencies are issued and controlled by central banks, which are responsible for managing the money supply and maintaining the stability of the financial system. They do this by setting interest rates and regulating the issuance of new money.

Cryptocurrencies, on the other hand, are decentralized and operate on a peer-to-peer network. They do not rely on a central authority to issue or regulate the money supply. Instead, they use blockchain technology to create a secure and transparent system for recording and verifying transactions. One of the main benefits of blockchain technology is its ability to create a secure and transparent record-keeping system. Because the blocks in a blockchain are linked and secured using cryptography, it is virtually impossible to alter or delete a transaction once it has been added to the chain. This makes it an ideal platform for storing and verifying financial transactions, as well as other types of sensitive data.

Another benefit of blockchain technology is its decentralized nature. Because it operates on a peer-to-peer network, there is no central point of control. This makes it resistant to censorship and tampering, as there is no single entity that can manipulate the data. This is particularly useful for cryptocurrencies, as it allows for the creation of a decentralized financial system that is not subject to the control of any one entity.

Cryptocurrencies also benefit from the speed and efficiency of blockchain technology. Because transactions are verified and recorded in real time, they are typically processed much faster than traditional financial transactions. This is particularly useful for cross-border transactions, which can take several days to clear using traditional methods. While the potential uses for blockchain technology are vast, it is still in the early stages of development and adoption. There are also a number of challenges that need to be addressed, such as scalability and security.

Despite these challenges, many experts believe that blockchain technology has the potential to fundamentally change the way we store and verify data, and to disrupt a wide range of industries.

Now, a lot of cryptocurrencies and exchange platforms use stablecoins. Stablecoins are a type of cryptocurrency that is designed to maintain a stable value, often pegged to a specific asset or currency. They are called "stablecoins" because they are meant to be less volatile than other cryptocurrencies, such as Bitcoin or Ethereum, which can fluctuate dramatically in value.

One of the main reasons people use stablecoins is to protect against the volatility of traditional cryptocurrencies. For example, if you own Bitcoin and its value suddenly drops, you could lose a significant amount of money. On the other hand, if you own a stablecoin that is pegged to the value of the US dollar, for example, the value of your stablecoin should remain relatively stable, even if the value of Bitcoin or other cryptocurrencies fluctuates.

There are several different types of stablecoins, each with its own unique features and characteristics. Some common types of stablecoins include:

1. Fiat-collateralized stablecoins: These stablecoins are backed by a specific fiat currency, such as the US dollar or the euro. They are called "fiat-collateralized" because they are backed by a physical asset (fiat currency) rather than by a digital asset like Bitcoin.

2. Crypto-collateralized stablecoins: These stablecoins are backed by a specific cryptocurrency, such as Bitcoin or Ethereum. They are called "crypto-collateralized" because they are backed by a digital asset (cryptocurrency) rather than by a physical asset like a fiat currency.

3. Non-collateralized stablecoins: These stablecoins are not backed by any specific asset or currency. Instead, they rely on complex algorithms and other mechanisms to maintain their stability.

Stablecoins have several potential benefits for teenagers and other individuals who are interested in using cryptocurrencies. For example:

1. Stablecoins can be a safer investment: As mentioned, stablecoins are designed to be less volatile than other cryptocurrencies, which means they are less risky to hold as an investment. This can be especially appealing to teenagers who are just starting to invest and may be more risk-averse.

2. Stablecoins can be exchanged for other cryptocurrencies, rather than cash, to further decentralize cryptocurrencies.

3. Stablecoins can be used for everyday transactions: Because stablecoins are designed to maintain a stable value, they can be used for everyday transactions, such as paying for goods and services or sending money to friends and family. This can be convenient for teenagers who want to use cryptocurrencies for everyday transactions, but don't want to worry about the value of their coins fluctuating.

4. Stablecoins can be used to hedge against market volatility: If you are concerned about the value of your traditional investments fluctuating, you can use stablecoins as a way to hedge against market volatility. For example, if you are worried that the value of your stocks might drop, you could invest some of your money in stablecoins as a way to protect against losses.

Stablecoins do have some potential drawbacks to consider as well. For example:

1. Stablecoins may not offer the same potential for returns as other cryptocurrencies: Because they are designed to maintain a stable value, they may not offer the same potential for returns as other cryptocurrencies, which can fluctuate dramatically in value. This means you may not be able to make as much money by holding stablecoins as you could by holding other cryptocurrencies.

2. Stablecoins may be subject to regulatory risks: Depending on the specific stablecoin you are using, it may be subject to regulatory risks. For example, if you are using a stablecoin that is pegged to a specific fiat currency, it may be subject to the same regulatory risks as that currency.

3. Stablecoins may be subject to counterparty risks: Stablecoins are issued by specific companies or organizations, which means they may be subject to short selling or bulk selling. This can cause the currency to have an artificial drop in price, such as what happened to the FTT coin.

Teenagers need to be careful about investing in cryptocurrency because it is a relatively new and unregulated market. There is no central authority overseeing the cryptocurrency market, which means that there is a higher risk of fraud and other types of financial crime. Additionally, because cryptocurrency is not regulated by any government or financial institution, there is no recourse if something goes wrong. This means that if you invest in a cryptocurrency, and it turns out to be a scam, or you get hacked, you may not be able to get your money back. When the hit Netflix show, *Squid Games*, rose to popularity, a new cryptocurrency called Squid Game coin rose to the scene. It started increasing in value due to the hype of the show and the strange premise of the coin—you had to play a game to get your coins. This was a novel concept and drew a lot of people in. The only problem, the game didn't exist. When people found out, the price of the coin tanked, and the people who had invested in the Squid Game coin ended up losing all their money.

In addition to the risks associated with cryptocurrency itself, there are also risks associated with the exchanges and platforms that allow you to buy and sell cryptocurrency. These exchanges and platforms may not have the same level of security and protection as traditional financial institutions, which means that there is a higher risk of your personal information being compromised or your funds being stolen. A good example of this is the fall of FTX.

Although I mentioned FTX earlier, it is good to discuss it more, because it teaches us a lot of lessons about the hazards of cryptocurrency. In 2017, MIT graduate Sam Bankman-Fried started a cryptocurrency-based hedge fund called Alameda Research. In 2019, he started the infamous cryptocurrency trading platform, FTX. The main thing that drew customers to FTX was that they could supposedly earn higher yields with FTX than with normal banks. This meant that by January 2022, they had gotten over $400 million in funding, with total funding of $2 billion, and the company's valuation reached more than $32 billion (more than Barclays or Dollar Tree). This allowed them to recruit big name celebrities like Kevin O'Leary, Stephen Curry, Tom Brady, Shaquille O'Neal, and many more. In fact, they even bought the Miami Heat Arena and re-named it the FTX Arena. Now, by this point you should know one of the biggest things about investing: What goes up must come down. For FTX, the downfall was the FTT coin. On November 2, 2022, Coindesk, a cryptocurrency news platform, published an article about the main asset of Alameda Research, FTT. It turns out, FTX was using FTT as collateral on the balance sheet. This means that they were tying all their assets to a cryptocurrency, which raised some red flags. On top of that, this coin was also particularly volatile, meaning that a decrease in price could ruin the firm. Upon the release of this article, Binance, FTX's main rival, decided to sell $530 million worth of FTT. The price of FTT plummeted, and FTX couldn't process customer requests to take their money out, since they didn't have the funds to fulfill the requests. This is known as a liquidity crunch. In seventy-two hours, FTX had paused all withdrawals, with Sam Bankman-Fried still trying to assure investors that everything was okay. Because the value of both Alameda and FTX dropped massively, Binance was getting ready to buy FTX but then realized all the illegal things FTX was doing. Some of these activities include mishandling of user funds, leveraging customer assets, and more. FTX filed for Chapter 11 bankruptcy. People who used the FTX platform are still waiting to recover their assets.

We can see from the fall of FTX how volatile the cryptocurrency market is. Unlike traditional investments such as stocks and bonds, which are backed by real assets, cryptocurrency is not backed by anything. This means that the value of cryptocurrency is largely based on speculation and the demand for it. If the demand for cryptocurrency decreases, the value of your investment could drop significantly. It is also important to be careful about investing in cryptocurrency because it is not a widely accepted form of payment. It may not be easy to use it to make everyday purchases or to pay bills.

As of 2019, you need to be at least eighteen years old in order to mine and invest in crypto. As mentioned before, cryptocurrencies are not backed by the government, meaning that you are investing at your own risk. There are several ways to invest in cryptocurrency, including:

1. Buying cryptocurrency directly: You can buy cryptocurrency on exchanges such as Coinbase or Binance using a credit card or bank account. There are more and more investing platforms coming up, so make sure to choose a reputable company.

2. Investing in cryptocurrency through a mutual fund or ETF: If you want to invest in cryptocurrency but are not comfortable buying it directly, you can invest in a mutual fund or ETF that tracks the value of cryptocurrency.

3. Mining cryptocurrency: You can also "mine" cryptocurrency by contributing your computer's processing power to the network and being rewarded with small amounts of cryptocurrency. However, this can be a complex and resource-intensive process and may not be suitable for everyone. Mining Ethereum is not possible anymore, since mining has been replaced by people who stake the Ether coins.

Now, we have discussed cryptocurrencies, but there is another digital asset that is storming onto the scene known as non-fungible tokens or NFTs. NFTs are a type of digital asset that represents ownership or proof of authenticity of a unique item or piece of content. They are built on blockchain technology, which allows them to be easily verified, tracked, and traded online.

One of the key features of NFTs is their non-fungibility, which means they cannot be easily replaced or exchanged for other items of equal value. This is in contrast to traditional cryptocurrencies like Bitcoin, which are designed to be interchangeable and can be easily exchanged for other goods or services. NFTs can be used to represent a wide range of items, including digital art, music, videos, and even physical objects. They can be bought and sold on online marketplaces, similar to the way in which traditional art or collectibles are bought and sold.

Another benefit of NFTs is that they provide a way for creators to establish ownership and control over their digital creations. In the past, digital content was often easily reproduced and shared without permission or compensation to the original creator. With NFTs, creators can sell unique copies of their work and receive payment for each sale. This has allowed young artists to sell their work as NFTs, allowing them to make a nice profit with their artwork. On top of that, musicians are starting to do the same, and it will only be a matter of time before more and more art becomes digital.

In addition to providing a way for creators to monetize their work, NFTs also offer a way for collectors and fans to own unique, one-of-a-kind items. This can be particularly appealing for fans of digital art, music, or other forms of digital media, who may not have had the opportunity to own a physical version of the item in the past.

There are several different types of NFTs, each with its own specific use case. Here are a few examples:

1. Cryptokitties: These are digital collectibles that represent virtual cats with unique genetic characteristics. They were one of the first successful NFT projects and helped to popularize the concept of non-fungible tokens.

2. Digital art: NFTs have been used to sell unique digital artworks, with some pieces selling for millions of dollars. This has been particularly popular in the world of cryptocurrency, where many people are interested in owning unique digital assets. Unfortunately, it is very easy for people to replicate the artwork by taking a screenshot or just taking a picture of the preview, so NFT

artwork is based on demand and not intrinsic value.

3. Physical objects: NFTs can also be used to represent ownership of physical objects. For example, a company called Lucidity has developed NFTs that represent ownership of car parts, allowing buyers to easily verify the authenticity of the parts they are purchasing.

There are several blockchain platforms that support the creation and trading of NFTs. Some of the most popular include Ethereum, EOS, and TRON. While NFTs have gained a lot of attention and have been the subject of much hype, there are also some criticisms of the technology. One concern is that the high price tags on some NFTs may be driven by speculation rather than the intrinsic value of the item. There are also concerns about the environmental impact of NFTs, as the blockchain technology that underlies them requires a lot of energy to operate. Running the servers needed to operate the blockchain requires massive amounts of electricity, making mining any cryptocurrency and storing it on the blockchain a difficult task to achieve sustainably. There are companies that are trying to power their servers using geothermal energy or solar power, but these are restricted to certain countries or regions. Lastly, while cryptocurrency may have seen record highs during the bull market following the pandemic, during the year 2022, we saw massive declines. This was mainly due to the fall of stablecoins like USD Coins. On the other hand, many countries and investors are still interested in cryptocurrency because of their promise of a decentralized finance system.

Decentralized finance, or DeFi for short, is a financial system that is built on top of blockchain technology. Blockchain is a technology that allows for the creation of a decentralized, secure, and transparent digital ledger. This means that it is not controlled by any one person or organization but rather is run by a network of computers.

One of the main goals of DeFi is to create financial services that are more accessible and inclusive, particularly for people who may not have access to traditional financial institutions. This includes people who live in countries where traditional financial institutions are not present, as well as those who may not have the necessary documentation or credit history to access traditional financial services. DeFi allows people to use cryptocurrency, such as Bitcoin or Ethereum, to access financial services like lending, borrowing, and exchanging currencies. These transactions are recorded on the blockchain, which means that they are secure and transparent.

One of the main benefits of DeFi is that it allows for the creation of financial products and services that are not controlled by any one person or organization. There is no central authority that can control the flow of money or manipulate the prices of financial products. Instead, the network is run by a decentralized group of computers, which means that it is more resistant to fraud and corruption. Another benefit of DeFi is that it allows for the creation of financial products and services that are more accessible and inclusive. For example, traditional financial institutions often have strict requirements for accessing their services, such as minimum balance requirements or credit history checks. DeFi allows anyone with an internet connection and a cryptocurrency wallet to access financial services, regardless of their credit history or financial status.

There are several different types of DeFi products and services that are available. For example, people can use DeFi to lend or borrow cryptocurrency, exchange one type of cryptocurrency for another, or even invest in cryptocurrency-based financial products.

One of the main risks of DeFi is that it is a relatively new and untested technology. This means there is a higher level of risk involved in using DeFi products and services, as there is a possibility that they may not work as intended. Additionally, the value of cryptocurrency can be very volatile, which means that the value of your investment may go up or down significantly over a short period of time.

Overall, decentralized finance is a system built on top of blockchain technology and designed to be more accessible and inclusive than traditional financial systems. While there are risks involved in using DeFi products and services, it has the potential to revolutionize the way that people access and use financial services, but as of right now, the technology is still in its infancy.

Chapter 6: The Young Savers Club

W hen you think of saving money, you probably think of putting it into a bank account or under your bed. Since ancient times, 90% of the population would do this, and for a lot of time, it worked. Wars, famine, and other historic events, however, made people lose trust in keeping all their money in one place. As time moved on, people put more and more of their money into banks and investments. Although there have been scenarios like the Great Depression of 1920, banks and investments have been the best way to save one's money. To provide more security, banks in the United States must hold a certain amount of money in reserves. That means that if you put $100 into a bank, at least $10 will be in reserves. The rest of your money will be loaned out to other people. When the bank collects interest on the money that they loan out, they will give you a very small slice of that interest, and whenever you need to withdraw your money, it should be available. You might now be thinking, "What happens if the bank doesn't have that money on hand?" The federal government will insure your deposit up to $100,000.

Earlier in the book, I talked a lot about inflation, so let's dive more deeply into it here. Before I get into the technical terms of inflation, I'll give a basic overview of it. Imagine you and a few other people are stranded on an island. On the island, there are two types of fruits, apples and peaches, with the same amount of demand for both. There are more apples than peaches, so naturally, the laws of supply and demand would make the peaches more valuable. So, people will try to acquire as many peaches as possible. Then a boat arrives, and they give the islanders many more peaches. This means that people are now going to perceive peaches as less valuable, since there are more of them. Now, imagine this in terms of money. Money as a whole is not valuable. A dollar bill is only worth a dollar because of the value we assign to it. This is known as intrinsic value. The paper to make the bill is probably worth only fifty cents, but we associate the dollar with a dollar's worth of value. So, coming back to inflation, if the government decides to print more and more dollar bills, then the value of the dollar will drop. So, inflation is the process of money losing its value.

You might be wondering how this relates to the money you have stored under your bed, but there is another way of explaining inflation: It is the increase of prices as a result of increasing purchasing power. So, as time goes on, your secret stash of cash will actually be worth less. To put it in numbers, if inflation is at a rate of 1.5% a year, then each year, your money is worth 1.5% less. Your bank account will still have the same amount of money, but it will have less buying power. This is one of the reasons why costs of living have increased so much after the pandemic. Most banks don't have interest rates high enough to offset inflation, therefore you need to keep your money in other places in order to combat inflation and grow your money. For a long time, bonds were the best way to do this. Bonds were very reliable and made enough returns to offset inflation, and they were available to a large variety of people. During the mid-20th century, the US government issued lots of bonds to fund the Cold War and other military efforts. Unfortunately, bonds started losing their return on investment, and interest rates started falling. Nowadays, there are ways you can save your money without losing it to inflation: high-interest savings accounts, stocks, real estate, retirement funds, and tax-free savings plans.

You've probably heard a lot about Swiss banks on the news and in pop culture. Many wealthy people put their money into Swiss banks because the Swiss currency is actually experiencing deflation. This means that the buying power of the currency is increasing (due to its strength against the euro). Therefore, it gives returns that can offset inflation. Swiss banks also offer lots of privacy as well. Now, if you aren't interested in putting your money in a Swiss bank, there are other ways you can save. A high-interest savings account is a financial product specifically designed to help individuals save money and earn interest on their deposits. These accounts are typically offered by banks and credit unions, and they often come with higher interest rates than traditional savings accounts. For teenagers, a high-interest savings account can be a great way to start building a strong financial foundation and learn responsible money management habits.

There are several benefits to opening a high-interest savings account for teenagers. First and foremost, these accounts offer higher interest rates, which means that the money deposited in the account will earn more money over time than standard accounts. This can be particularly beneficial for teenagers who are just starting to save and may not have a lot of money to deposit. The higher interest rate can help their savings grow faster and give them a sense of accomplishment as they see their money grow. Another benefit of high-interest savings accounts for teenagers is that they can help teach financial responsibility. By opening a savings account, teenagers can learn the importance of setting financial goals and working towards them. They can also learn about budgeting and how to manage their money wisely. For example, they may decide to set aside a certain amount of money each month to save for a specific goal, such as a car or a college education. In addition to the financial benefits, high-interest savings accounts can also provide a sense of independence and autonomy. By being able to manage your money and make financial decisions, you can gain a sense of security about your future. This will be especially important for you as you start to save up for things like higher education.

In conclusion, a high-interest savings account can be a great financial tool for young investors. They offer higher interest rates, which can help you grow your savings faster and learn responsible money management habits. There are a lot of banks that offer high-interest savings accounts, so it is up to you in order to find the one that works for you. These accounts can provide you with 4-8% annual interest, so depending on the rate of inflation, you might even be able to make money just by leaving it in the bank. You will also have the compound interest, so you might not have to worry about inflation after all. It is important to consider the fees associated with the accounts—a lot of companies offer high interest rates, but then they also have massive fees attached to them, meaning that you might make more if you opt for an account with a lower interest rate but also lower fees.

Some people may not be eligible for these high-interest bank accounts, but there are other ways you can save and invest for the long run. Long-term investing in the stock market can be a highly effective way to grow wealth over time, especially if you are investing in a diverse portfolio of stocks. However, it is important to have a well-thought-out strategy in place in order to maximize your chances of success. Here are some key considerations for developing a long-term investing strategy in the stock market:

1. Diversify your portfolio: Diversification is key to reducing risk in your portfolio. This means investing in a variety of different stocks and asset classes, rather than putting all of your money into one or two stocks. One way to diversify is to invest in an index fund, such as the S&P 500, which tracks the performance of 500 large-cap stocks. This can help to spread risk across a wide range of companies and industries.

2. Set clear goals: Before you start investing, it is important to have a clear understanding of what you are trying to achieve. Do you want to save for retirement, pay for college, or build wealth for other long-term goals? Your investment strategy should be tailored to

meet your specific goals. Make sure your goal is realistic and not over your skill level.

3. Develop a long-term investment plan: A long-term investment plan should outline how much you will be investing each month, what types of investments you will be making, and how you will be monitoring your portfolio. You should review and revise this plan regularly to ensure that it is still aligned with your goals. If you just want to make as much money as possible, you will have a different plan than someone who is trying to save up for their kids' college. Different plans may require different savings and index funds as well.

4. Monitor your portfolio regularly: It is important to regularly review your portfolio to ensure that it is performing as expected and to make any necessary adjustments. This may include rebalancing it to maintain the desired asset allocation or selling off underperforming stocks and replacing them with better performers. If your strategy

always stays the same, chances are you are not earning as much as you could. Companies that used to be blue chips are now underperforming, and other companies that were once considered bad investments are now performing very well.

5. Consider the impact of taxes: Taxes can have a significant impact on your net returns, so it is important to consider the tax implication of your investments. For example, long-term capital gains taxes are generally lower than short-term capital gains taxes, so it can be beneficial to hold onto investments for longer periods of time in order to take advantage of these lower tax rates.

6. Be prepared for market fluctuations: The stock market is known for its volatility, and it is important to be prepared for ups and downs. It can be tempting to panic and sell off your investments when the market takes a downturn, but this is often not the best course of action. Instead, try to remain focused on

your long-term goals and stay the course.

Throughout this book, I have been talking a lot about compound interest, so now is the best time to fully explain it. If you have been through math class, you probably know what a linear function is; it is when something increases or decreases by a constant amount. Think of it like a taxi fare, where there is a base cost, and then you pay extra depending on how far you travel. Compounding functions are a bit different, because your rate of change will increase or decrease exponentially. Now, you might be wondering, "Why is compound interest so powerful?", and for that, we need to look at the numbers.

Saving money isn't just about putting it in the right place—time also matters. You might have heard the phrase, time is better than timing. This means that the amount of time you spend in the market is more important than the time when you enter the market.

Let me give you an example: During the 2008 recession, some people were annoyed that their investments were starting to turn blood-red, and they sold all of them, hoping that they would at least recoup some of their losses. Unfortunately for them, by the time the recession had ended, and the stock market reached all-time highs, they missed out because they hadn't spent enough time in the market to benefit from the recovery. This is one of the most common mistakes that people make when they are investing. They pull out too early, and then complain that the market or whatever they are investing in isn't good. In fact, many of the same people who complain that investing is too complicated or not lucrative enough are also the same people who end up working until they become eligible for senior citizens discounts. The fact of the matter is that when you are investing in anything, you need to be patient. If you've been on any social media platform, you have probably seen the massive number of get-rich-quick schemes, or the many people encouraging you to invest in the most obscure things. A truly successful investor has to be able to wade through the ups and downs of the market, or else their profits will crumble as easily as they made them.

Unfortunately, compound interest can also destroy you as well. I'll give you an example. When people were trying to start businesses in my home city in India, they would often take loans to get enough money to start their business. Since competition was fierce, people took on more loans in order to make their business stand out. This included things like having a fish-tank window. (This did actually happen.) When the banks called on the businesses to pay back their loans, people were surprised to see that they had to repay more than they thought. This is because the interest associated with the loans had compounded. Now, during the early 2000s, many people took advantage of easy loans to buy houses or other expensive things they could not have afforded otherwise. When they had to pay back their loans, they found their interest had compounded. So, whether you are trying to leverage your bets or finance a car, you need to be able to pay back your interest on time, or else you will have to face the extra interest. As a young person, it might be tempting to apply for many different credit cards and feel as though you are essentially getting free money. For example, I knew a person who decided to get a student-friendly credit card back when he was in university. He ended up maxing the card out, and when it was time for him to pay the money back, he couldn't do so. He ended up having to apply for another credit card to pay back the first one, and so on. When he left university and got a decently paying job, he was finally able to pay back the interest he owed, and he thought he would not need to worry anymore. Unfortunately, when you are late in paying back your interest, your credit score drops. Therefore, he couldn't get any of the more powerful credit cards, he couldn't get loans for a car or house, and spent years paying everything back. Your credit score matters a lot, and one of the biggest mistakes that people make is taking it for granted. As high schoolers, we have to be careful about any debt we take on.

In economics, there is a common term called the business cycle. Essentially, this is a tool that economists use to roughly predict the ups and downs of the market. Now, realistically, economists haven't always been the most accurate, but there are some actions of the government that can help you gauge what the market will do.

When the GDP of a nation goes up, we all assume it's a good thing. Unfortunately, there is a side effect of this growth— inflation. When an economy is coming out of a recession, the government will essentially have to spend lots of money to bring the economy back up; this is called an expansionary policy. The government will typically buy bonds to gain the capital necessary to grow the economy. When they buy these bonds, investors receive cold hard cash, which they will then invest in other businesses, and so on.

This stimulates the economy by introducing new money into the market, raising inflation. The government may also take on debt to fund things like infrastructure, schools, military, and more things that require government spending.

The government could also decrease taxes to allow people to put more money in the economy. This raises inflation until it gets too high. When this happens, the government will enact a contractionary policy. Essentially, this is the government putting the brakes on the economy to slow down inflation. When this happens, the government will sell its bonds, ease government spending, and increase taxes. This will then put the economy back into a recession. The whole recession will play out before the economy goes back to normal. So, you can see how there is no real thing as perfect timing because the market will go up or down, no matter what you do. So, you might as well save or invest your money. That way, you can at least be prepared for a rainy day.

Saving money doesn't mean just putting it in a bank account; it can also be spending it smartly. You probably know people who have a lot of credit cards.

When I was in middle school, I wondered why they would pay all those yearly fees. Then I realized that credit cards often give you benefits and rewards compared to debit cards. Since credit card companies make a lot of money from interest payments, they can give people with good credit scores a lot of benefits. Since most people don't know about these benefits, the card issuers can take advantage of that and pocket the extra money. The pro users, on the other hand, use the benefits to the point that they actually receive more in rewards and points than the worth of the card.

Sometimes, it's the little things that allow us to reach our financial goals. Instead of buying that coffee from Starbucks, we might invest in Starbucks itself. You just need to do some simple math to figure out how much money that cup of coffee is taking away from you. In the US, a cup of coffee costs, on average, $5. If you buy just one cup a day, you are spending about $35 a week. Per month, you are spending about $140 on coffee, about $1,680 per year. Now, if you invested that money into an index fund that gives you, on average, a 5% return, then per year, you would be earning about $84. Five years later, assuming you reinvest your gains, you would make $434 on top of your original investment. And since your profits would continue to compound, the monetary gains would outweigh the loss of caffeine in the morning.

The reason why wealthy people end up leaving so much money behind is because of generational wealth. The rich often don't work for their money; they end up creating it. When someone goes to work and gets paid, that's working for money. When someone creates something that makes them money, without them having to constantly work on it, that is creating money. High schoolers like us need to find ways to create money. In the beginning of the book, I mentioned that it was no longer adequate to work a normal, middle-class job and still be able to maintain a family. This is why places like California are facing such high poverty levels. Even if you earn a little less than six figures, it still won't be enough to cover your cost of living in that state. Many people say that the solution to problems like these is to tax the people with more money. That way, that income can be used to provide services to the middle class. Unfortunately, one of the most iconic states in the US has already tried this and is facing a harsh reality.

You probably know the state of California for its amazing landscape, iconic cities, Silicon Valley, Hollywood, and great education. This is why so many people moved there. It simply provided an atmosphere that doesn't exist in many places around the US. As the population grew, so did the taxes. The state realized that if they could tax the high-income earners heavily, then they could use that money to address public crises, like water shortages, homelessness, failing educational systems, and more. Unfortunately, the people who were basically carrying the state on their shoulders realized something: If we can work from anywhere, why do we live in a place that is taxing us so much? Thus began the great exodus from California. Companies like Tesla, Oracle, and Hewlett-Packard (HP) have all left the state for places where the taxes are much lower, like Texas. Then people who were earning a lot of money and paying those massive taxes also started to leave. In fact, more than 40% of the state's tax revenue came from these millionaires and businesses (Hepler, 2021)[5]. This means that the state's infrastructure is now crippled. Public schools are no longer receiving the funding they once did. Measures to ease homelessness have been reduced, and the problems the state has been battling continue. These problems will only increase as California keeps the tax rates high. People who are suffering say that the solution to their problems is to tax the remaining affluent people. These people, who are now being given the burden, will also leave the state, thus continuing the cycle.

---

[5] Hepler, Lauren. "What's Driving California's Mass Exodus?" *Www.youtube.com*, CNBC, 23 Jan. 2021, www.youtube.com/watch?v=Ez90rXhMWjE.

Being in the middle class and still struggling is more common than people realize. When my sister was applying to colleges, she found that any college outside the state was going to cost, on average, $50,000 a year just for tuition. Our family was earning more than the threshold to receive scholarships, but not enough to consider the cost of college a minor expense. There are people who are earning too much to receive food stamps but have to decide whether to buy vegetables or pay rent. People who receive aid from the government end up not receiving the funds in time, don't know how to get the services they need, are in a position where they are unable to receive those services, and the cycle of poverty continues. In the beginning of Chapter 2, I mentioned how the most famous quote in the movie *The Wolf of Wall Street* was, "I want to solve your problems by becoming rich!" The harsh reality of our society today is that we need to be rich in order to live a decent life. The world has become the survival of the richest. Over twenty years ago, when my dad first started his career, his salary was 8,000 rupees, or $1,840 a year. To put it into perspective, that monthly salary today wouldn't even cover the cost of a nice dinner for our family and relatives. When my dad was making that, however, he was able to live a decently comfortable life and still managed to save some money. I'm not saying this to scare anyone or to suggest that money can make you happy. It is just to say that good financial habits and savings are necessary to lead a comfortable life. The market moves in cycles, what goes up will come down, so you need to be prepared for any storm.

One of the biggest cancers to our society is the idea that you can get rich without having to work for it. Although some people may have been fortunate enough to be born into a wealthy family, the majority of us reading this book are going to have to provide for ourselves.

Chapter 7: Storied Pasts

T hroughout this book, I have given you a ton of tips and ways to achieve financial independence as a high schooler. Yet, you might ask me, "If you're also a high schooler, why should I listen to you? Aren't there better people to teach me?"

To answer those questions, I'll give you a story. One of my close friends (yes, I have friends) was telling me how he wanted to get a new car before he went to college. He said that he picked up a job at McDonald's to help pay for it. His neighbor offered his old car for $10,000. On top of that, my friend's parents offered to pay half of the cost. In his eyes, it was a better idea to work every day of the summer at McDonald's, having a customer throw a drink at him, cleaning the bathrooms, and so much more, than to learn how to invest. When I asked him why he didn't want to invest, he told a long story. The day before school ended, his dad said that instead of paying $5,000 for the car, he would give his son the $5,000 in cash, and he wanted him to invest that money to pay for the car. He didn't want to listen to his parents, because he thought they had done this only to prevent him from getting his own car, going wherever he pleased, and gaining his freedom. He didn't know that if he had put his money into the S&P 500, that year alone, he could have made an extra 25% return on his investment. Throughout the summer, he had managed to make $3,000 at the cost of missing out on a fun vacation. He is still trying to save up for his car, and he wishes he had listened to his parents. The point I'm trying to make is that as a teenager, you are probably not inclined to listen to your parents or teachers; you are more likely to listen to your friends and people of a similar age. You are more likely to take suggestions for your next pair of Jordans from your best friend than from your dad.

To answer that second question, there are definitely people more qualified than me to teach you. This book is merely a vehicle for me to try to teach you the topics that these grown-ups have found. If you aren't going to listen to them, it might be better to at least learn how they made their fortunes through investing.

To start things off, let's go with the legend Warren Buffett. While you might imagine him as an old man who is basically living off of compound earnings, he is one of the best examples of long-term investing. Many people who are big in the world of investing came about very recently, but Warren Buffett is ninety-three years old. In his lifetime, he invested in major companies right when they were started—Apple, Microsoft, Xerox, and countless others. He has donated millions of dollars to charities and other organizations across the globe. Although he is one of the richest people alive, he leads a pretty simple life. He lives in an old house, he drives an older car, he doesn't have a smartphone, and he drinks a lot of Cherry Coca-Cola. Warren Buffett is best known in the investing world for his company; he bought Berkshire Hathaway, which was originally a textile company, to be able to invest in other companies. What business insiders refer to as a float is what keeps Berkshire Hathaway afloat.[6]

---

[6] All information used in the Biography of Warren Buffett is from his Biography and the following sources.

Overcast, Kimberly. "Warren Buffett's Investment Strategy." *Investopedia*, 31 August 2023, https://www.investopedia.com/articles/01/071801.asp .

Buffett, Warren. *Warren Buffett: the Life, Lessons and*

Buffett used the company's insurance subsidiaries' "float" to fund the purchase. These insurance subsidiaries collected premiums from policyholders but did not have to pay out all claims immediately. This created a pool of money (the float), which could be invested until claims needed to be paid.

Buffett took advantage of this float, using it as a cheap source of financing instead of using his own money or borrowing from banks to buy more shares of Berkshire Hathaway. This allowed him to acquire a larger and larger stake in the company without depleting his personal resources.

As Buffett gained more control over the company, he transformed it from a textile manufacturer into a diverse conglomerate. He used the company's profits and cash flow, as well as the float generated by the insurance subsidiaries, to acquire other businesses and stocks. This strategy allowed him to compound his wealth significantly over time.

Rules for Success. Independently Published, 2017.

Floats also enabled Berkshire Hathaway to quickly acquire and revitalize companies struggling with short-term problems. With Fruit of the Loom, that is exactly what happened. In 2002, after the company's stock had lost 97% of its value, Berkshire paid $835 million to acquire the struggling clothing business. Dividends are an investor's secret weapon, according to Benjamin Graham (not quoted), Buffett's mentor. Apple, Coca-Cola, and American Express, to name just a few of the Fortune 500 companies in which Berkshire Hathaway holds significant stakes, have a track record of paying dividends that are either maintained or grow year over year. For fifty-five years straight, Coca-Cola, for instance, has increased its annual dividend. When Warren Buffett was eleven years old, he bought his first stock from his father, who was a stockbroker. Using the profits he made from that stock, at the age of fourteen, he bought forty acres of land and rented it out. It was very clear that he was no ordinary kid; he was destined for a great future. When it was time for college, his father urged him to go to the University of Pennsylvania, one of the best business schools in the world. However, he decided to transfer to the University of Nebraska, a decision that few people would make. One thing to note about

Warren Buffett is that he values value. Unlike other investors who want to make a quick buck, Buffett is willing to wait years to make massive profits. When he graduated, he went to study under the legendary value investor Benjamin Graham. Graham basically created the concept of value investing. During the Great Depression, he lost most of his fortune, teaching him to value stocks carefully. Buffet learned a lot from Graham, and in the more recent editions of Graham's book, *The Intelligent Investor*, Buffet wrote a foreword about the lessons he learned from him. Even though the two were very similar, Warren Buffett had one big difference: He also looked at companies' management and their products' competitive advantage.

This has allowed him to invest in companies like Apple, long before it was the behemoth we know today. Even day-to-day investors can use this strategy. If you focus on a company's products and management, you can identify strong companies with good numbers over weak ones. The strategy allowed Buffett to invest in many undervalued companies before investors realized their values and drove the price up. Warren Buffett is now a billionaire and is still part of Berkshire Hathaway and many charitable organizations. He has taught us that making money often requires years of experience and patience. In a world where people make easy money, Warren Buffett shows us that it often takes hard work to make good decisions and lead a life of great success. He has earned the title "The Oracle of Omaha."

While Warren Buffett has seen market crashes that rewrote history books, Mark Cuban faced two market crashes that completely redefined investing. He had very humble beginnings. He was born into a middle-class family in the Pittsburgh area, and he first made money by selling coins and stamps. This was an early sign that he would become one of the most influential business people of all time.[7]

By the 1990s, the internet had started to revolutionize the way the world worked. As the prices of computer hardware and software dropped, and the technology grew

---

[7] All information used in the Biography of Mark Cuban is from his Biography and the following sources.

Cuban, Mark. *How to Win at the Sport of Business: If I Can Do It, You Can Do It.* Diversion Publishing Corporation, 2013.

"Mark Cuban - Age, Education & Shark Tank." *bio. Biography.com*, https://www.biography.com/business-leaders/mark-cuban .

more powerful, millions of companies started to move their services online. If you wanted to buy an airline ticket to India before the internet, you had to pay a travel agent to book the ticket and hotel accommodations. Now, you can go to a website like Expedia and book your tickets, hotels, activities, and more. Mark Cuban witnessed the rise of the internet and heavily monetized it.

In 1982, Cuban was a graduate of the University of Indiana, Bloomington. He had been fired from his job as a salesperson for the popular retailer, Your Business Software. At that time, the internet was not treated as an all-encompassing tool for businesses. Back then, most software came on floppy disks sold at stores. To give you context, most computers in the 1980s and '90s could probably hold five or six word-processing documents before they ran out of storage. It was this world that Mark Cuban entered. After he was fired, he joined another Indiana University graduate and started working at Audionet. Audionet was a primitive version of today's Twitch. Audionet, however, faced the dot-com boom, arguably one of the most interesting finance bubbles of all time.

This was a period of excessive speculation and investment in internet-related businesses in the late 1990s and early 2000s. The dot-com bubble, which lasted from 1995 to 2000, was characterized by a surge in the stock market and initial public offerings (IPOs) of internet-based companies. The stock market grew rapidly, and many internet businesses went public, some achieving valuations of billions of dollars. The bubble was driven by the belief that the internet would revolutionize the way people do business, leading to unlimited growth and profits. As a result, enthusiasm for the technology sector was high, and venture capital firms and investors were willing to invest in any technology company with a good idea and a website. As more companies went public, their stock prices skyrocketed, creating a bubble in the market. This meant that entrepreneurs who had no idea what they were doing started internet companies that were just glorified tax benefits. Therefore, when the bubble burst, thousands of internet companies went bankrupt, their stocks falling to single digits. Mark Cuban might well have been one of the victims of this crash, but he managed to survive it.

When Broadcast.com (previously Audionet) was still riding high, Cuban realized that the boom would not last forever. So, he decided to sell Broadcast.com in exchange for some Yahoo stock. Since he knew Yahoo's share value would decline when the bubble burst, he sold most of his stock just a few months before the crash. He realized over $1.1 billion dollars in profit from the sale and managed to keep his fortune safe amidst one of the biggest market crashes in recent history. Although you could say that he benefited from lucky timing, it is hard to ignore the fact that his market experience allowed him to know the best time to pull out. Mark Cuban's story is a good example of how investing is something you need to be actively involved in. You can't just expect to make money by doing nothing, and anyone telling you that is probably wrong. Mark Cuban's story illustrates that investing requires amazing foresight, but the story of Jordan Belfort teaches us that sometimes, foresight can end you.[8]

[8] All information used in the Biography of Jordan Belfort is from his Biography and the following sources.

Reiff, Nathan, and Timothy Li. "Who Is Jordan Belfort, the Wolf of Wall Street?" *Investopedia*, https://www.investopedia.com/investing/who-is-jordan-belfort/ .

Belfort, Jordan. *The Wolf of Wall Street*. Bantam Books, 2007.

As I mentioned before, Jordan Belfort's story has been widely popularized by the movie *The Wolf of Wall Street*. Unfortunately, the actual banking regulatory structure back then was a lot more relaxed. You see, the banking laws before the crash of 2008 were less strict and allowed people like Jordan Belfort to make the system his slave. The stock market's regulations typically tighten only when people break them or find a loophole, so that should give you an idea of how lax the banking laws were then. Jordan Belfort worked at a bank before he got laid off after Black Monday, an infamous stock market crash that occurred on October 19, 1987. It was the largest one-day percentage drop in the Dow Jones Industrial Average in its history, with the Dow dropping 22.6% and losing 508 points. The crash was caused by a combination of factors, including a combination of computerized sell orders, program trading, an overvalued stock market, and international instability. Jordan Belfort was still a fresher in the finance world, before the floodgates opened. So, in order to continue to stay afloat, he decided to get a job trading pink sheets. To explain it simply, pink sheets are stocks that are not worth enough to be on any major index like the NASDAQ or NYSE. Therefore, there were fewer regulations on them, and the companies were more sketchy. The main benefit was that the stockbrokers could make a 50% commission on them. So, Jordan Belfort used his Wall Street skills to sell clients thousands of dollars worth of penny stocks, making them think that they had hit gold. This made him a lot of money, even though he wasn't a part of a big financial institution. The main problem was that the clients he was selling to were not particularly wealthy; they didn't have much to invest. This is a common problem that many entrepreneurs find themselves in, even me. Although selling fidget spinners was a great way to make some pocket money, I found early on that I wouldn't become a millionaire by selling them. This is why a lot of investors want to invest in startups—they have more potential for growth.

Knowing this, Jordan Belfort had a choice: either reinvent himself and find a new business or continue this charade of poor investments. If you watched the movie, you know he chose the latter. He founded the company Stratton Oakmont, a name that he chose to sound established and reliable. He hired some salespeople and taught them sales tactics that would get even the most astute investors to buy worthless penny stocks. This allowed him to scale up his business massively, making tons of money in the process. Now, although this would have been good enough for most people, Belfort knew that he wanted greener pastures.

Jordan Belfort had a vision for success, and his spirited ambition drove him to take Steve Madden, a footwear company that he believed could be transformed into a powerhouse, to IPO. Belfort, who had a knack for spotting trends, saw the potential in the company's line of casual shoes. He recognized the growth potential and felt it was the perfect opportunity to make a big splash on Wall Street. With Belfort at the helm, the company grew exponentially. He drove Steve Madden to increase its production, expand its markets, and engage in aggressive marketing. Under his leadership, the company went public and raised millions of dollars. It was a remarkable feat, and it was all made possible by Belfort's vision. His charisma and confidence inspired those around him, and his business acumen was unmatched. He knew exactly how to take a company from startup to IPO, and his knowledge and drive helped him to make it happen. But unfortunately, the good times would soon come to an end.

The SEC began investigating Belfort and his firm in 1996 in response to allegations of securities fraud, stock manipulation, and money laundering. Belfort and his partner, Danny Porush, had been engaging in fraudulent activities such as insider trading and market manipulation to make huge profits for themselves and the firm. The SEC was concerned that these activities would lead to a crash in the stock market and wanted to make sure that investors were protected from potential losses. The investigation uncovered a wide range of evidence to support the allegations, including evidence of large amounts of money being transferred from Stratton Oakmont to the partners' personal accounts for their own use, such as making large purchases and taking expensive trips. As a result of the investigation, Belfort and Porush were indicted on a variety of fraud-related charges and were ultimately found guilty. The SEC also uncovered evidence of Belfort and Porush using Stratton Oakmont's funds for personal use, such as making large purchases and taking expensive trips. They had been using Swiss banks to hide their currency and hiding money in any way possible. At the end, the empire that Belfort had built came crashing down because of the greed and mismanagement. The biggest thing we can learn from Jordan Belfort is never to break the law and hope not to be caught.

We often associate brands with people— Phil Knight and Nike, Steve Jobs and Apple— but Vanguard is an example of a company that doesn't need that type of introduction. Investment firms like Berkshire Hathaway have made their mark in the markets for many years, but Vanguard has been around only since 1975. In that time, they have managed to make their mark on the investing world like no other company ever before.

The Vanguard Group is an American investment firm founded in 1975 by John Bogle. It is now one of the world's largest investment companies, managing over $5.2 trillion in assets. Bogle had the idea of creating a mutual fund that tracked the S&P 500 index. In 1976, Vanguard launched its first index fund, the Vanguard 500 Index Fund. The fund tracked the S&P 500 index, and was designed to provide investors with a lower-cost, diversified portfolio that could match the performance of the stock market as a whole (Bogel, John C)[9]. In the early years, Vanguard was a small company and was struggling to gain traction. Bogle was an advocate for index investing and pushed for the concept to become mainstream. Despite the low cost of Vanguard's funds, investors were slow to invest in them. This often happens with new companies, since people are reluctant to trust their money to newcomers in the market. However, in the early 1980s, Vanguard began to see some success. Bogle's idea of index investing had become more widely accepted, and investors were beginning to see the benefits of investing in Vanguard's funds. Even today, index funds are some of the safest and best long-term solutions for keeping your money secure. Unlike most companies at the time, Vanguard wanted to keep customer money safe, rather than invest it in risky bets. By the mid-1980s, Vanguard had become one of the largest and most successful mutual fund companies in the United States.

---

[9] Bogle, John C. *Stay the Course: The Story of Vanguard and the Index Revolution.* Wiley, 2018.

During this period, Vanguard continued to expand its offerings. In 1981, the company launched the Vanguard International Value Fund, which was designed to provide investors access to international markets. In 1982, the Vanguard Total Stock Market Index Fund, which was designed to track the performance of the entire US stock market, launched. This was huge, as in the past, you would have needed weeks to do something that computers could now automate in minutes. In the late 1980s, Vanguard introduced its first index-based exchange-traded fund (ETF), the Vanguard Total Stock Market ETF. Nowadays, thousands of people invest in ETFs, and it is hard to imagine investing without them. Vanguard had already created a name for itself in the investing world, but the hits would continue. In 1988, the firm launched its first actively managed fund, the Vanguard Capital Opportunity Fund. This fund was designed to provide investors exposure to growth stocks. The beauty of this was that the Vanguard name now allowed people to invest in stocks that they would have previously not have considered. By the end of the decade, Vanguard had become one of the largest and most successful mutual fund companies in the United States (Bogel John C)[10].

In the early 1990s, Vanguard launched its first bond fund, the Vanguard Total Bond Market Index Fund, which was designed to provide investors exposure to the entire US bond market. Many people pay little attention to bonds because of their relatively low return, but for people trying to invest in the long run, bonds can be a lifesaver in terms of a reliable source of cash flow. In 1991, Vanguard launched the Vanguard Diversified Equity Fund, providing investors exposure to a diversified portfolio of stocks, bonds, and other asset classes. In 1995, the Vanguard Total International Stock Index Fund provided investors exposure to the international stock market. By 1996, Vanguard launched its first sector funds, focusing on specific sectors of the stock market. This concept is pretty common nowadays, but back then it was highly unusual to invest in specific industry sectors without being an expert yourself. In the late 1990s, Vanguard also launched its first international bond fund and its first money market fund. The company also began to offer 401(k) plans and other retirement products at the same time. These products were a major driver of Vanguard's growth.

[10] Bogle, John C. *Stay the Course: The Story of Vanguard and the Index Revolution.* Wiley, 2018.

In 1999, Vanguard launched its first online brokerage service. This was a major step forward and marked the beginning of the firm's move towards digital services. In 2003, the first robo-advisor, a digital service that provides investors automated, low-cost financial advice without needing to speak to a human advisor (Bogleheads)[11].

Vanguard is successful for a few reasons; for one, they are not very actively managing their clients' portfolios. Instead, they track the performance of various market segments rather than trying to beat the market through active management. The firm also provides guidance and education to help investors achieve their long-term goals. This means that big-time investors, who have a lot of capital to invest, will be able to maintain their gains. Vanguard's success can also be attributed to their corporate structure. Vanguard doesn't own the funds; rather, the funds own Vanguard. Therefore, the shareholders own the company. This means that almost all the profits are returned to the shareholders, which creates a more positive atmosphere for people to

[11] Bogleheads. "The Vanguard Group." *Bogleheads*, https://www.bogleheads.org/wiki/The_Vanguard_Group.

invest in. In the world of finance, there are so many stories of people betraying their customers and lying to their investors, but Vanguard stands as one of the few companies that is able to beat the stereotype and provide consistent performance.

Next, I want to touch upon something that happened very recently. This was a financial crisis that changed the landscape of investing and finance forever, and it shows how the market can give and take. This crisis led to many new laws that protect our financial institutions, and it influenced the world beyond just the borders of the United States. The crisis also shows how computers changed the world of investing and made it even more interconnected. If you haven't caught on yet, I am talking about the 2008 financial crisis, which was immortalized in the film, *The Big Short*, based on a group of short sellers who ended up making billions from the crisis. Although some people made money, many more lost everything. Even people who had nothing to do with the financial markets suffered. The crisis is the perfect example of how corporate greed and corruption has a way of becoming a monster that can no longer be controlled. So without further ado, let's get into it.

Our story starts way before the crisis actually begins, during the 1960s and '70s, when banking wasn't a profession you chose because you wanted to be rich. Instead, you wanted job security and a stable income. However, in 1987, investment bank Drexel Burnham Lambert employee Michael Milken created the Collateralized Debt Obligation (CDO). Milken was known as the "King of Junk Bonds." You might remember from earlier in the book that bonds usually don't typically offer high returns. However, junk bonds, which have higher risk, pay higher interest rates. The bond issuer might default on their payment, and you lose all your money, but Milken's junk bonds were often tied up with things like mortgages and other securities, where people usually pay back on time. He figured out that he could bundle a bunch of these junk bonds into one big bond, meaning that the investors—and most importantly Milken himself—could make a massive profit compared to normal bonds. As you can imagine, others started pouncing on this once-in-a-lifetime opportunity (Hollar, Sherman).[12]

[12] Hollar, Sherman. "Michael Milken | Biography, Junk Bonds, Pardon, & Facts." *Britannica*, https://www.britannica.com/biography/Michael-R-Milken .

Most people invested in CDOs because they could make a lot of money but also because they were seen as a safer alternative to the stock market or real estate. Around that time, banks realized that mortgages were a great way to bundle CDOs. This started a wave of many people with bad credit ratings or too little money for a down payment buying houses. Usually when people buy houses, they don't have all the money upfront, so they make a down payment and pay the rest in installments. But in this case, the banks started offering mortgages to people who did not have a sufficient down payment or were not able to meet their monthly installments. The banks could charge these people a higher interest rate on their loans, meaning that people who invested in those loans as bonds could make a higher return. The only problem was that if people defaulted on their loans, the banks would be dead in the water and would have to pay out the remaining money on the bonds to the people who had bought them.

Another problem was that most people investing in these CDOs did not know what bonds comprised them. They just assumed that people would always pay their mortgage, so their investment would be safe. However, if you looked closer at the CDOs, you would realize that a lot of the bonds inside them were horrible, and the borrowers hadn't paid their mortgage in months or years. Normally, if a bond issuer does this, ratings agencies give the asset a bad rating, warning investors about the risk of investing in the asset. The problem was that big banks were paying the ratings agencies bribes to artificially increase the ratings of these CDOs. Therefore, most retail investors didn't know what they were getting into. This caused a bubble in the housing market, which had devastating consequences. Investors often have trouble spotting a bubble in the market because the media tends to act as if everything is fine. Similarly, many were skeptical that the housing market could collapse because they always thought it was too big to fail. Unfortunately, history has told us that everything can fail, and investors should approach everything with a healthy dose of skepticism.

As the market continued over-valuing the CDOs, the bubble became bigger and bigger, meaning that when it popped, the financial system reeled. People who wanted the opportunity of a lifetime realized that it would only be a matter of time before people began defaulting on their mortgages, causing the banks to hemorrhage money. When the bubble did burst, banks could no longer give customers their money and people lost their homes. Many started withdrawing massive amounts of money from their bank accounts as they feared for the worst (Council on Foreign Relations).[13]

This caused the share prices of banks to drop massively, meaning that people stopped investing in them, causing them to almost fail. Luckily, the US government was able to bail out a lot of the banks, but Lehman Brothers went bankrupt in an explosive way.

Unlike other banks, Lehman Brothers had massive stakes in these subprime mortgages. As you might imagine, this scenario drove their stock extremely high before the crash. Unfortunately for them, the market started to show cracks in 2007, so by

---

[13] Council on Foreign Relations. "Timeline: The U.S. Financial Crisis." *Council on Foreign Relations*, Council on Foreign Relations, https://www.cfr.org/timeline/us-financial-crisis .

that point, the company was radically overvalued. When the crisis started, the stock fell so sharply that the company had to cut 1,200 jobs from its mortgage division, showcasing the beginning of the end. Most companies would have gotten rid of their CDOs, but Lehman Brothers instead bought more, causing the price to go back up since investors still thought CDOs were safe. Another red flag was that the earnings for 2007 weren't as strong as they should have been, so investors should have let go of their holdings, yet Lehman Brothers continued assuring investors that everything was fine. This caused the bubble to grow even more. By the end of 2007, the firm had to start buying back stock at a 42% premium. This essentially meant they were trying to bolster some investor hope and stabilize the stock price. But it was too little too late. The stock plunged 77% in the first week of September, and hopes that a Korean firm would buy Lehman Brothers were also quickly extinguished. The stock then dropped another 45% as a result.

At that point, Lehman was facing a $3.9 billion loss, and they had to accept defeat. For example, they had to write down $5.6 billion worth of assets. A write-down is essentially when a company decreases the value of their holdings to try and balance their losses. For example, let's say you buy a car for $10,000. You expect that the car will be worth $8,000 in two years. But after two years, you find out that the car is only worth $5,000. You have to write down the value of the car on your books by $3,000 because you expected it to be worth $8,000, but it's only worth $5,000 now. The credit rating agencies also started getting on their tails, and the only way for Lehman Brothers to avoid getting downgraded by the ratings agencies would be to sell parts of the firms to partners.

By September 12, 2008, Lehman Brothers had $1 billion left in cash and were struggling to find other options. During that weekend, Bank of America and Barclays tried to take over the bank but were unsuccessful. By the time Lehman declared bankruptcy, the stock had plunged over 98%, one of the biggest drops in history. The CEO later remarked that the government should have also bailed out Lehman Brothers as well as the other banks(Lioudus, Nick).[14]

---

[14] Logan, Michael. "The Collapse of Lehman Brothers: A Case Study." *Investopedia*,

After the Great Depression, the US government realized that if banks were to fail, it would have massive, long-lasting impacts on the country, especially if banks were deemed "too big to fail." When a bank is too big to fail, it essentially means that the bank controls so much money that its collapse would have devastating impacts on the economy. This can be especially problematic if a bank decides to merge with others, as it reduces competition in the marketplace. So, if a bank were to fail, the US government would take over the bank, pay back the customers of the bank and their deposits, and help the bank get back to business.

Even though this saved the US economy from falling into a similar depression in 2008, a lot of people are annoyed at this practice for a few reasons. For starters, it basically means that the banks get only a slap on the wrist for causing grievous economic damage. During a recession, divorce rates, suicide rates, dropout rates, heart disease rates, and murder rates all

https://www.investopedia.com/articles/economics/09/lehman-brothers-collapse.asp .

increase—and the only punishment for a bank's risky behavior is a fine. Also, the cash the government uses to bail out banks comes from taxpayer money, which also annoys people, as they don't want to encourage the bank's risky behavior. Usually, if a bank is about to fail, another bank will buy it. Banks do not want the economy to worsen, so they would rather just buy up whatever is left of the other bank. The government bails out banks if they are about to fail, not just if they have a bad earnings report. This is a two-sided issue that politicians have fought for a long time, and it goes back to the Great Depression, when the government saw the first-hand effects of too little regulation.

The oldest story that I will share is from the early 20th century. This was a time before cell phones or email were invented, so information traveled a lot slower. In fact, the term stock ticker comes from a piece of machinery that printed the price of stocks on a long sheet of paper with information from a telegraph. Only wealthy people had access to technologies like this. The car was just starting to become popular, and in some parts of the country, electricity was still not common. This gives you an idea of how far back the Great Depression happened.[15]

After World War I, the United States entered a period called the Roaring '20s. This was when music, technology, and politics entered a renaissance after the war. At this time, businesses saw massive profits that were greater than those before the war. Therefore, the market was on a rampage, with profits and stock prices soaring more than anyone expected. This is also where we get the term bull market, because the market was like a rampaging bull. The government was not too involved in banking or the stock market as they had other things to worry

[15] All Citations Pertaining to the timeline and happenings of the Great Depression.

Chen, James. "Liberty Bonds: What They are, How They Work." *Investopedia*, https://www.investopedia.com/terms/l/liberty-bond.asp .

Federal Reserve Bank of St. Louis. "What Caused the Great Depression? | St. Louis Fed." *Federal Reserve Bank of St. Louis*, https://www.stlouisfed.org/the-great-depression/curriculum/economic-episodes-in-american-history-part-5 .

"Financial Reforms." *FDR Museum*, http://www.fdrlibraryvirtualtour.org/page05-03.asp. Accessed 12 September 2023."Great Depression | Timeline." *Britannica*, https://www.britannica.com/summary/Great-Depression-Timeline .

Office of the Historian. "Milestones: 1921–1936 - Office of the Historian." *Milestones: 1921–1936 - Office of the Historian*, United States Government, https://history.state.gov/milestones/1921-1936/great-depression .

about, like prohibition (a period in US history when alcohol was banned).

Now, as we all know, what goes up will come down. Yet, there was a problem—the banking system at that time was not prepared for the coming down part. By 1928, there was a massive amount of speculation in the market, which caused many people to invest on leverage, meaning that if the price of their investments went down, it would be over. Also, many people sold wartime bonds, otherwise called Liberty Bonds, in exchange for more volatile assets like stocks.

People had very few liquid assets, as they thought they could beat inflation with stocks. This all meant that if the market crashed, it would result in billions of dollars vanishing from the financial system. It also meant that the people who were investing on margins would have to pay back their loans, and if they couldn't, banks would run out of reserve cash.

The market finally crashed by the end of 1929, in an event known as Black Thursday. Stock prices crashed, and investors sold a record 12.9 million shares to try and recover their losses. However, there was an even bigger problem—the banks were about to crash.

You see, if you deposit $100 into the bank, the bank actually doesn't hold the $100. Instead, they will loan out the money to another bank or individual, collect interest, and give some of the interest back to you. This means that the bank may only have 5% to 10% of your money at hand. Therefore, in an event like the Great Depression, when many people tried to withdraw their money at once, the banks could not do so, and they collapsed.

At that time, there were no required reserves. Nowadays, banks have to hold a certain amount of your money in reserve so the bank can manage withdrawal requests. The big problem is that during the Roaring '20s, many banks had few reserves, causing them to fall flat when people started withdrawing their money.

Larger banks sold their assets, whereas smaller banks went out of business, leaving people penniless. With depositors unable to access their savings, it became a massive issue—people couldn't pay off the loans they had used to buy stocks, the loan companies lost millions of dollars, and so on. To recover some of their losses, the banks fired massive numbers of people. The people who lost their jobs were struggling because no places were hiring. To make matters worse, there was a massive dust storm in the Midwest, causing many farming communities to lose their harvest. This caused people to move west, to California.

Since the US was a major power in the world's economy, the Great Depression had effects that went beyond the US as well. In Germany, they were still paying back reparations from World War I when the depression hit. Since the German government could not afford the payments, they decided to print more money, which caused hyperinflation. This caused Germany to spiral out of control, leaving many people unemployed. This crisis inspired a painter by the name of Adolph Hitler who was rejected from art school to start a revolution in his country, you might have heard of him. In the United Kingdom, industrial and agricultural output decreased as they had lost a lot of their financial backing in the United States.

The Soviet Union, which was transitioning into an industrialized economy under Stalin's rule, faced significant challenges during the Great Depression. The country's agricultural sector struggled, and industrial production declined, causing hardship for many Soviet citizens.

The US found ways to recover from the Great Depression. For one, the government started massively improving the nation's infrastructure as a way of giving people more jobs. Companies received money from the government to open back up. It also helped that World War II stimulated the economy; more industrialization and people purchasing more Liberty Bonds allowed the economy to mostly recover. Once the 1950s rolled in, the effects of the Great Depression were largely over, and the United States economy was back under control.

One of the major impacts of the Great Depression on the 21st century is the establishment of social safety net programs. In response to the widespread poverty and unemployment during the Depression, the US government implemented various measures to provide assistance to those in need. Programs such as Social Security, which provides retirement benefits, disability insurance, and survivor benefits, were created to protect vulnerable individuals and promote economic stability. These programs continue to play a crucial role in the lives of millions of Americans, safeguarding them from economic hardships.

The Great Depression led to the implementation of stricter financial regulations to prevent another stock market crash and banking collapse. The SEC was established to regulate the stock market, ensuring transparency, fairness, and investor protection. The Glass-Steagall Act separated commercial and investment banking, preventing excessive speculation and reducing the risks associated with banks' involvement in the stock market. These regulations aimed to promote stability, maintain public trust, and prevent a recurrence of the financial chaos.

Moreover, the Great Depression influenced the role of the government in managing the economy. Prior to the Depression, the prevailing economic theory emphasized limited government intervention and laissez-faire policies. However, the severity of the crisis challenged this belief and led to a reevaluation of the government's role in stabilizing the economy. Keynesian economics, advocated by economist John Maynard Keynes, gained prominence during this period, arguing for active government intervention through fiscal and monetary policies to stabilize the economy and stimulate aggregate demand. This shift in economic thinking had a profound impact on subsequent economic policies, with governments around the world adopting measures to manage the business cycle and mitigate the impact of recessions.

In the 21st century, the US government has taken several actions to prevent another Great Depression-like event. In response to the 2008 financial crisis, the government implemented various measures to stabilize the economy and prevent a collapse of the financial system. The Troubled Asset Relief Program (TARP) was enacted, providing financial assistance to troubled banks and other financial institutions. The Federal Reserve employed unconventional monetary policies, such as quantitative easing, to inject liquidity into the economy and lower interest rates. These actions were aimed at restoring confidence in the financial markets and promoting economic recovery.

Furthermore, the Dodd-Frank Wall Street Reform and Consumer Protection Act, passed in 2010, aimed to enhance financial regulation and prevent excessive risk-taking by financial institutions. It established stricter oversight of banks, introduced new rules on derivatives trading, and created the Consumer Financial Protection Bureau to protect consumers from abusive financial practices. These regulatory measures were put in place to prevent a repeat of the risky behaviors and lax oversight that contributed to the 2008 financial crisis.

Moreover, the US government has been vigilant in monitoring economic indicators and taking proactive measures to address potential risks. The Federal Reserve closely monitors inflation, unemployment rates, and other economic indicators to make informed decisions about monetary policy. Government agencies, such as the Department of Treasury and the Council of Economic Advisers, provide analysis and advice to guide policy making and help maintain economic stability.

It is not important to know the specific measures taken by the government to prevent the next big depression. Rather, it is important for us to know what to do when one happens and how to prevent ourselves from losing money with it. When the market does go south, the best advice is very simple: Do not panic. As I have mentioned before, time in the market beats timing, therefore the losses you incur during a downturn will be temporary. The market always has a way of resolving itself, so don't panic.

The other thing you can do is to keep at least some of your assets liquid. Although the thought of inflation eating up your money is hard, if the market does go south, it will be beneficial to have some cash on hand. This will also give you some peace of mind during a recession if you have lost your main source of income. Many financial advisors recommend that you have savings to cover at least three months of your normal spending. Do this, and your main question will not be "How can I afford rent?" but rather, "How can I continue to invest?"

This is how recessions can create millionaires. People who continue to invest, even when the market is down, are more likely to get the benefits of capital gains once the market goes back up. This is why during the 2008 recession, many real estate investors started to aggressively buy properties with whatever money they had. Once the market started going back up, they would either list the properties for sale at a higher price, or they would rent the properties out, enabling them to pay back their loans and reinvest into other properties.

Recessions are also perfect for testing out ideas. For example, during the dot-com bubble, a lot of small internet companies were wiped out. Companies that did not have a strong foundation or workforce often failed, especially when they were being tested by unfavorable market conditions. If a company can survive a recession, it confirms that they likely have the skills to weather another one. Recessions tend to weed out companies that have shady practices, since government regulations become much stronger after recessions, and more regulations are created. So as always, there is a bright side to a recession. It may be harsh, but it is still there.

Chapter 7: Storied Pasts

Conclusion

This book has covered a lot of topics, from stocks to crypto, so the conclusion will summarize the chapters and the main topics discussed in each. It will also give you the essence of some of the lessons we can learn.

In Chapter 1, we learned about assets and liabilities. Assets are things that can increase in value and continue to provide value after the initial purchase. Liabilities decrease in value, and lose a lot of their value after their initial purchase. In Chapter 1, we also discussed some of the different asset classes, such as stocks, bonds, real estate, and cryptocurrency.

In Chapter 2, we discussed stocks. We learned that stocks are small pieces of a company you can own. The value of a stock depends on a company's performance and earnings. The chapter also went over ETFs, mutual funds, options, and more.

Conclusion

In Chapter 3, we learned about the field of real estate, or the buying and selling of properties. We discussed house hacking, the rental market, and how to get a real estate license. Many states have a minimum age limit of eighteen, and you might have to go to a pre-licensing class, but it is a good résumé boost, and it provides you with an alternative job.

In Chapter 4, we learned about bonds and annuities. Bonds are the promises to pay back loans with interest, and the money you can make from bonds is the interest associated with the loans. Annuities are a type of bond that gives you a fixed interest rate, which may be low and require a large lump-sum investment.

In Chapter 5, we learned about cryptocurrency. Cryptocurrencies are digital currencies that can be exchanged for other cryptocurrencies or cash. Stablecoins are cryptocurrencies with a set value; the main purpose is to serve as an exchange to other cryptocurrencies. Cryptocurrencies are stored on the blockchain, which is a digital ledger that stores all the transactions of the cryptocurrency.

In Chapter 6, we learned about the different ways to save money. We covered retirement accounts and the importance of financial independence. We also discussed some of the different ways we can save money in our day-to-day lives.

Well, this is it. If you have made it this far, I would first like to thank you. It takes a lot of dedication to learn this much about a particular subject. Personal finance is complicated, and I have tried my best to make it easy to understand. I wrote this book because I wanted young investors to know the basics and to gain insights on topics that you might not learn at school. As a student, both me and my teachers know that a lot of the information we are taught is not going to affect our day-to-day lives. Some of the work we are assigned can be easily automated, and companies know that.

With the advent of generative AI tools like ChatGPT, it is hard to predict the future and what sorts of jobs we might have. Analysts have already predicted that the vast majority of jobs that currently employ people will soon be automated. That is a very scary thought, and it forces us to ask ourselves, "How can I continue to pay for my necessities?" Even high-paying jobs are nowadays not enough for most people, since they do not have the necessary financial skills to manage their money. More money won't solve the problem for them; it will just make the problem worse.

In the beginning of the book, I mentioned that some of my friends do not really care about the importance of personal finance, as they think it is not relevant to them. The fact of the matter is that the minute you enter college, you already start accruing debt, and you have to start figuring out your future. One of the best pieces of advice I have been given is that it is never too early to think about what you want to do later in life. It allows you to not only figure out your career, but the more time you spend on it, the more confident you will be about your decision. If you don't feel confident, you still have time to modify your plan. For example, one of my good friends went to college and studied finance and political science. People might wonder why he chose that combination, but it was actually genius. During the summer, he found an internship at a finance company and worked there for a few months, making some good money. Later, he realized that he did not like the field and wanted to pursue something else. He pivoted towards law, and with his political science experience, he was able to score well on his LSAT and get into a good law school. When I first started high school, I wanted to become a doctor, but after exploring the field, I realized that it was not for me. I then asked myself why I wanted to go into a STEM field. It wasn't because I had a passion for science but rather because I had a passion for the salaries. That is why I doubled down on my passion for finance and economics. If my motivation is to use the financial system to my advantage, then why not just study it?

This book is called *The Young Investors Club* because there aren't too many resources for people who are just getting started. Most of the resources are for people who are already making money and need to invest it. This book is for the people who just want to learn what to do once they get into a financial position where they can start investing. Start building your financial empire now, and you can one day stand back and gaze at its majesty.

About the Author

Skandha Suhas Badrinarayan is a teenager who lives in Portland, Oregon. He currently attends Westview High School, where he was introduced to the world of investing and personal finance by his accounting and economics teachers. For the past three years, he has also been the Founder and President of the Oregon Young Investors Club, a club that seeks to teach teenagers about investing and personal finance. His work in the club inspired him to write this very book. Additionally, he is a DECA State Champion and has qualified for the international level of the competition. His internships at Venture Capital and Real Estate companies have given him a firsthand look at how corporate and small businesses operate. In his free time, he is a competitive typist, ranked in the top 5% of the world, he also enjoys performing kirtan, and playing badminton with his friends.

https://www.linkedin.com/in/skandha-suhas-badrinarayan/

September 2023